THE *CROSSROADS* PROGRAM

Crossroads is a church school program for seventh and eighth graders that has been developed by Faith Alive Christian Resources.

The broad goals of the *Crossroads* program and of the other courses for seventh and eighth graders are as follows:

1. To encourage students to reflect on their own relationship to Christ and to see how that relationship affects their daily activities—a very specific goal of this course on relationships.

2. To acquaint students with great biblical themes (such as kingdom and covenant), equipping them with Bible-study skills, helping them practice biblical teachings, and encouraging them to develop good Bible-reading habits.

3. To acquaint students with the history and faith of the church, helping them acquire and use a basic "faith vocabulary" common to the Reformed tradition, enabling them to see the relationship between doctrine and life, and encouraging them to participate fully in the life and work of the church.

4. To help students deal with such critical areas as identity, freedom, responsibility, authority, morality, faith, and ethics—all within an integrated biblical, confessional, and historical framework.

During most class sessions your child will be working with other seventh and eighth graders through a Scripture study in the student book that remains in the classroom from week to week. (Ask your child to share the book with you at the end of this course.) What you will see at home each week is a tear-out sheet containing the memory work and a set of devotional readings and reflections that reinforce the Scripture study done in class. You can help your seventh or eighth grader by asking about the lesson, encouraging memorization of the selected passages, and incorporating the weekly devotionals "From Monday to Saturday" into your family worship time.

A word about the memory work policy for *Crossroads* courses: Young people are generally encouraged to memorize longer passages of Scripture rather than a different, isolated text each week. You'll notice from the chart on pages 2 and 3 that your child will be memorizing 1 John 4:7-12 during the next twelve weeks.

As you can see, we depend on you, the family, to make church school everything it can and should be. Your involvement in this aspect of your child's life will reinforce the significance of your relationship with your child. Thank you for your interest and cooperation.

Crossroads courses:

A.D.: A Study of Church History

Believe It or Not: A Study of Prophecy

Honest to God: A Study of the Psalms

One of a Kind:
     A Study of Christian Identity

Family Ties: A Study of the Covenant

Fit to Follow: A Study of Discipleship

Live It!: A Study of James

Connecting: A Study of Relationships

Lesson	Scripture	Lesson Truth	Memory Work (from NIV)
7 Front and Center?	Matthew 20:20-28	When we know God, we seek to live a life of humility and service for his sake.	Dear friends, since God so loved us, we also ought to love one another. 1 John 4:11
8 More Stuff?	1 Kings 21:1-16	When we know God, we can trust him to meet our needs and to help us be content with whatever we have.	Review 1 John 4:7-11
9 Trust Me!	Acts 5:1-11	When we know God, we seek to build honest and trusting relation-ships.	Review 1 John 4:7-11
10 Short Fuses	Jonah 4	When we know God, who is loving and slow to anger, we want to express our anger in a healthy way that will not harm ourselves and others.	Review 1 John 4:7-11
11 Just a Flashy Coat?	Genesis 37:1-36	When we participate in or approve of violence, we destroy the dignity of others and our sense of community. When we know God, we try to live in peace with others and work against violence.	No one has ever seen God; but if we love one another, God lives in us and his love is made complete in us. 1 John 4:12
12 A New Life	Colossians 3:9-10, 12-17	"If we love one another, God lives in us and his love is made complete in us" (1 John 4:12).	Review 1 John 4:7-12

Lesson	Scripture	Lesson Truth	Memory Work (from NIV)
1 Through My Father's Eyes	Psalm 139:1-16	When we can praise God for the wonderful person he has made each of us, we can develop happy and healthy relationships with others.	Dear friends, let us love one another, for love comes from God. 1 John 4:7
2 Family Ties	Luke 15:11-31	God places us in families so that we may learn about him and grow closer to him.	Everyone who loves has been born of God and knows God. 1 John 4:7
3 Friends Forever	John 12:1-8	When we love each other we are obeying God's command "Love each other as I have loved you" (John 15:12).	Whoever does not love does not know God, because God is love. 1 John 4:8
4 Many Are One	John 4:1-26	God intends for us to live in harmony with people who are different than us.	This is how God showed his love among us: He sent his one and only Son into the world that we might live through him. 1 John 4:9
5 Choices	1 John 2:15-17; Philippians 4:8-9; Matthew 15:19	God has placed us in the world, but he does not want us to love the things of this world.	This is love: not that we loved God, but that he loved us and sent his Son as an atoning sacrifice for our sins. 1 John 4:10
6 Take Notice!	Luke 16:19-31	When we know God, we seek to live a life of awareness and compassion for his sake.	Review 1 John 4:7-10

A Study of Relationships

Connecting

For the Family

Dear Family:

For the next twelve weeks your child will reflect on the significance of relationships in our lives. On pages 2 and 3 you'll find the course (*Connecting: A Study of Relationships*) outlined to give you a quick overview of each week's lesson theme and Scripture study.

We trust that these lessons will help your child think about who he or she is in God's eyes. We'll examine the role of family and friends in our lives as we reach out and interact in the larger society and culture we live in. We'll also see how relationships are often hurt by pride and greed and other selfish behaviors. It is our genuine hope that your child will grow and experience God's love changing hearts and strengthening relationships—connecting to God and to others because God is love. The goals for this course are as follows:

1. Your child will recognize that self-acceptance and peace come with seeing ourselves through God's eyes.

2. Your child will develop a greater appreciation of the importance God places on the role of the family in his or her personal growth.

3. Your child will realize that God intends us to establish caring and supportive friendships, and that he wants us to reflect his love for us.

4. Your child will realize that in order to live together as God wants us to live, we need to accept each other.

5. Your child will be motivated to make wise choices with respect to our culture.

6. Your child will examine the effects of ignorance, pride, greed, dishonesty, anger, and violence on our relationships to others, to the world, and to God.

7. Your child will demonstrate God's love in his or her relationships as he or she starts living a new life in Christ.

For general information about the *Crossroads* program and how you can help at home, turn to page 4.

The Editors

CONNECTING

A Study of Relationships

Bible Crossroads

FAITH
ALIVE®
Christian Resources

Grand Rapids, Michigan

Acknowledgments

The Education, Worship, and Evangelism Department is grateful to Arie Knoester for writing this *Bible Crossroads* course. Knoester is a high school teacher at Grand Rapids Christian High School, Grand Rapids, Michigan.

We are also grateful to Tim Foley, Paul Stoub, Edwin de Jong, and Dan Spoelstra for illustrating this textbook.

Unless otherwise noted, Scripture passages are taken from the HOLY BIBLE, NEW INTERNATIONAL VERSION, © 1973, 1978, 1984, International Bible Society. Used by permission of Zondervan Bible Publishers.

Scripture passages noted from the NIrV are taken from the HOLY BIBLE, NEW INTERNATIONAL READER'S VERSION, © 1994, International Bible Society. Used by permission of Zondervan Publishing House.

Scripture passages noted from THE MESSAGE are taken from THE MESSAGE, © 1993, 1994, 1995. Used by permission of NavPress Publishing group.

Scripture passages noted from the NCV are taken from THE HOLY BIBLE, NEW CENTURY VERSION, © 1987, 1988, 1991 by Word Publishing, Dallas, Texas 75039. Used by permission.

Faith Alive Christian Resources published by CRC Publications. *Bible Crossroads* series. *Connecting: A Study of Relationships,* student book, © 1996 by CRC Publications, 2850 Kalamazoo Ave. SE, Grand Rapids, Michigan 49560.

We welcome your comments. Call us at 1-800-333-8300 or e-mail editors@faithaliveresources.org.

ISBN 1-56212-172-3

5 4 3 2

Contents

Through My Father's Eyes

I WISH . . .

Aram stood on the track, waiting for the start of the fifty-yard dash. It was the day of the middle school track meet, and Aram felt amazingly confident. He just knew he would beat the three other eighth graders who waited with him. He felt like a cannonball ready to fire!

A few months ago he wouldn't have been so confident. Because back then he had been a skinny wimp. He couldn't find his muscles if he tried. "I wish there was some magic that would change the way I look," he often thought. And then one day, leafing through his stack of comics, he'd come across an ad. It featured a stunning picture of a man bulging with muscles. "You Too Can Look Like This," promised the ad.

Aram was amazed to read that the

man—Lionel Strongfort—had once been weak and puny too. For just a few dollars, said the ad, you could find out the secret of Mr. Strongfort's well-muscled body. "Why not?" Aram thought. And he mailed off some of his hard-earned paper-route money.

When the package finally arrived, Aram was a little disappointed. Strongfort's "secret" was strangely simple: get up early, exercise, get lots of fresh air, eat good wholesome food. None of this was exactly news

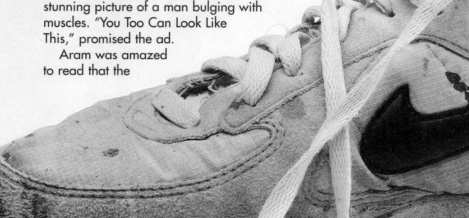

to Aram—he'd known it all before. But now he was desperate enough to give it a try.

Following the program was hard work, especially at first. Many times Aram almost gave up. But he managed to keep up a pretty good routine. He knew he'd never look anything like Lionel Strongfort, but he did manage to put on a few pounds, and he felt great. Now he was ready to show his friends the "new" Aram.

Afterwards, Aram described the race:

The time came at last for me and three other athletes . . . to go to our marks, get set, and go; and I did, in a blind rush of speed which I knew had never before occurred in the history of athletics. It seemed to me that never before had any living man moved so swiftly. Within myself I ran the fifty yards fifty times before I so much as opened my eyes to find out how far back I had left the other runners. I was very much amazed at what I saw. Three boys were four yards ahead of me and going away.

It was incredible. It was unbelievable, but it was obviously the truth. There ought to be some mistake, but there wasn't. They were ahead of me, going away. . . .

The race was over. I was last by ten yards. Without the slightest hesitation I protested and challenged the other runners to another race, same distance, back. They refused to consider the proposal, which proved, I knew, that they were afraid to race me. I told them they knew very well I could beat them. . . . When I got home I was in high fever and very angry. I was delirious all night and sick three days.

My grandmother took very good care of me and probably was responsible for my not dying.

PHONY

Using words, create a "portrait" of the kind of teenager portrayed in magazine ads or on TV (or, if you prefer, draw a picture instead).

- How does the media portrayal of the "ideal" teen make you feel?

- What kind of personal problems can develop when we feel pressure to be an ideal person?

- "What am I worth?" is a question we often let others answer. How dependable are other people's answers compared to God's answer?

Let no one deceive you with empty words.
Ephesians 5:6

ON-LINE

In Psalm 139 the psalmist uses a different brush and different colors than the world uses to paint a picture of who we are. We are original designs created by the Master designer, God the Creator!

1. God knows the subject of his portrait. Note the key words (**bold** type) in verses 1-4 on page 8. What does God know about us? What does he know about our activities? Our thoughts? Our words?

2. God uses special techniques to study his subject. Visualize these techniques described in verses 5-10 (in **bold** type). Your teacher will help you demonstrate each of them with your classmates. Imagine God knowing all about you as he

   - hems you in . . .
   - lays his hand upon you . . .
   - guides you with his hand . . .
   - holds you fast with his right hand . . .

3. God selects unique materials—check out his supplies in verses 13-16. Read the words in **bold** type and picture cells, organs, joints, muscles, bones. . . .

4. God creates a masterpiece—you! Now it's your turn to stand back and admire his handiwork! Put the key phrases in verse 14 (**bold** type) in your own words. List as many words as you can think of to describe God's wonderful work.

¹O LORD, you have **searched me**
   and you **know me.**
²You know when I sit and when I rise;
   you **perceive my thoughts** from afar.
³You **discern my going out and my lying down;**
   you are familiar with all my ways.
⁴Before a word is on my tongue
   you **know it** completely, O LORD.

⁵You **hem me in**—behind and before;
   you have **laid your hand** upon me.
⁶Such knowledge is too wonderful for me,
   too lofty for me to attain.
⁷Where can I go from your Spirit?
   Where can I flee from your presence?
⁸If I go up to the heavens, you are there;
   if I make my bed in the depths, you are there.
⁹If I rise on the wings of the dawn,
   if I settle on the far side of the sea,
¹⁰even there your **hand will guide** me,
   your **right hand will hold me** fast.

¹¹If I say, "Surely the darkness will hide me
   and the light become night around me,"
¹²even the darkness will not be dark to you;
   the night will shine like the day,
   for darkness is as light to you.
¹³For you created my **inmost being;**
   you knit me together in my mother's womb.
¹⁴I praise you because I am **fearfully and wonderfully** made;
   your **works are wonderful,**
   I know that full well.
¹⁵My **frame** was not hidden from you
   when I was made in the secret place.
When I was woven together in the depths of the earth,
   ¹⁶your eyes saw my **unformed body.**
All the days ordained for me
   were written in your book
   before one of them came to be.

Psalm 139:1-16

8

Search me, O God, and know my heart; test me and know my anxious thoughts.

Psalm 139:23

MY PORTRAIT

Sometimes, especially as we're growing into adulthood, it is easy to have anxious thoughts about ourselves—how we look, what others think of us, what we do well and not so well. Accepting ourselves and liking ourselves as God's masterpiece is part of growing up. In this exercise, you'll be "drawing" a self-portrait by completing a personal inventory.

Step 1: Inside the photo frame on the left, write down some of your weaknesses. You might consider the following areas of your life:

- physical appearance
- personality
- relationships with others
- school performance
- special abilities such as music or sports
- relationship to God

It's OK to have certain things you don't like about yourself. After all, nobody's perfect! But it's *not* OK to go around hating yourself for your weaknesses. That hurts! When your list is complete, put an X by each item that you have the power to change. Put a ♡ by those you'd like to ask God to help you accept.

Step 2: In the photo frame on the right list your strengths. You may find this harder to do than listing your weaknesses. Maybe you'll even think it's like bragging. But your strengths are just as much a part of you as the things you'd like to change about yourself. Look at the areas listed under Step 1 and write down things you like about yourself. Think of qualities you admire in other people you love, and write down those you have too. Don't forget to mention the strengths others have noticed you have. Then star one or two that you feel are your strongest traits.

WONDERFUL WORKS: A PRAISE LITANY

All: I praise you because I am fearfully and wonderfully made; your works are wonderful, I know that full well. I praise you, O Lord, for I am wonderfully made.

Group: A painter uses his paint and brush, a potter uses his hands and clay, a carpenter uses a hammer and nails, and God used his gracious love to create a masterpiece.[1]

Leader: God created that masterpiece when he created you!

There is no one else exactly like you! You are a very valuable work of art.

My wish for you is that you can truly appreciate the *you* God created you to be![1]

Group: Before I had a name, God knew me. I am [say your first name quietly].

Leader: Before you were born, God knew you would be someone's son or daughter, a sister or brother, a cousin, a friend. But most of all, God knew you would be his child.

All: God made us. He created us to belong to Christ Jesus. Now we can do good things. Long ago God prepared them for us to do.

Each One: [quietly] Thank you, Lord, for your love to me. I am your child. Help me to show this love to others.

All: We praise you, O Lord, for we are wonderfully made.

[1]jacket copy, *Sandi Patti and the Friendship Company* by Sandi Patti, © 1989, Word Inc.

Family Ties

BEAVER AND COMPANY

"You're goofy, Beaver!" That's Wally talking to his brother Beaver on the 1950s television show *Leave It to Beaver*. When their dad raises his voice to check their mischievous, usually innocent pranks, the two immediately obey. "Boy, he really gave us the business," says Wally. When their mother calls them in for supper, the entire family sits around the table and enjoys the delicious meal she's spent her day preparing. Everybody has something nice to say, including "please" and "thank you."

CORBIS-BETTMAN

Does this sound like a real family to you?

People living in North America during the '50s loved watching family shows like *Ozzie and Harriet* and *Father Knows Best*. Even in the '70s, the *Brady Bunch* played the perfect family, and Bill Cosby managed to be "Dad of the Year" in the '80s. These families got along well. Their problems were fairly simple, and they always had happy solutions. Everyone knew they weren't real families, but everyone liked to pretend they were. Today, some parents and children still try to make their family look like one of those "perfect" families on TV.

THEN AND NOW

Families and family life have changed quite a bit since the 1950s. Following are some general descriptions of typical '50s families and their lifestyles. Read through the list and circle the things that have changed for your family and other families you know.

- Most families look the same: dad, mom, and several kids. Small families are uncommon.

- Dad is the family breadwinner. He works all day and comes home, eats the supper his wife serves, and reads the newspaper. Dad's the boss, the final word on important decisions.

- Mom stays home during the day. Her job is to clean the house, cook the meals, and take care of the kids. She's the one you go to if your feelings are hurt or you skin your knee. She's the one who'll give you tender loving care.

- The whole family eats supper (and often breakfast and lunch) together. Children are expected to be polite at the table and finish whatever's on their plate.

- Eating out is a rare luxury and a real treat. Each kid gets to order a hamburger, some fries, and a milk shake at the cafe or maybe at the drive-in with carhop service.

- On Sunday the neighborhood is pretty quiet. The stores on Main Street (there aren't any malls!) are closed. Everyone seems to be taking it easy, reading, sleeping, visiting.

- Kids looking for excitement and adventure can watch cowboy stories like *The Lone Ranger* and *Roy Rogers* on the black-and-white television in the living room.

- Many parents don't like rock 'n' roll music. Some say the communists are using that kind of music to corrupt our youth.

- In school, the teacher's always right. If kids get into trouble at school, they'll also be punished at home.

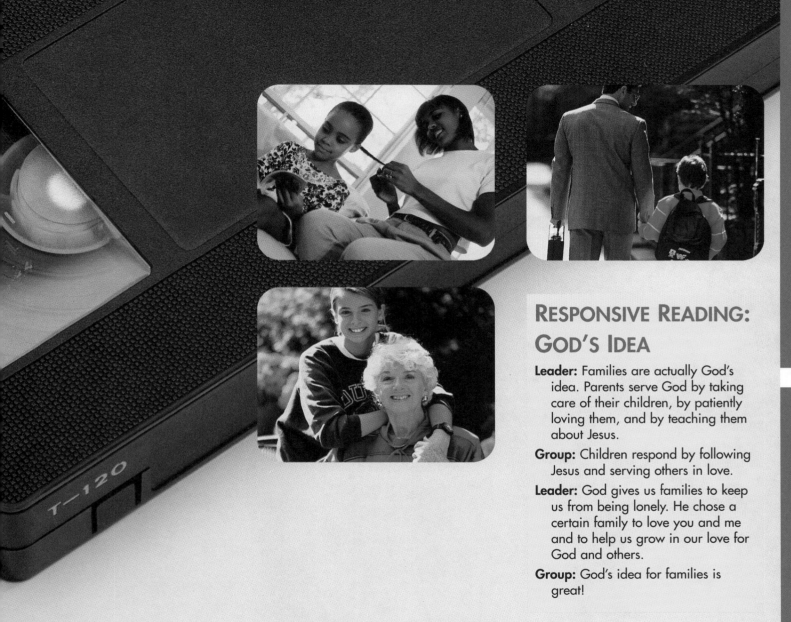

RESPONSIVE READING: GOD'S IDEA

Leader: Families are actually God's idea. Parents serve God by taking care of their children, by patiently loving them, and by teaching them about Jesus.

Group: Children respond by following Jesus and serving others in love.

Leader: God gives us families to keep us from being lonely. He chose a certain family to love you and me and to help us grow in our love for God and others.

Group: God's idea for families is great!

LOVE WINS

Families have been broken by sin ever since the fall of Adam and Eve. Our Scripture passage today tells the story of one family with broken relationships, and it shows how love can triumph over problems. More than that, it's about our heavenly Father's love for us, his sinful children. Read the part of the Scripture passage you are assigned, and then tell the story to the rest of the group in your own words.

ACT 1: AT HOME
(Luke 15:11-12)

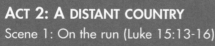

ACT 2: A DISTANT COUNTRY
Scene 1: On the run (Luke 15:13-16)

ACT 2: A DISTANT COUNTRY
Scene 2: Headed home (Luke 15:17-20)

ACT 3: BACK HOME
Scene 1: Welcome (Luke 15:20-24)

ACT 3: BACK HOME
Scene 2: Angry feelings (Luke 15:25-31)

ON-LINE

1. Did the father really want to divide his inheritance? What would you have done in his place?

2. What plans had the younger son already made when he asked his father for his share? How did his feelings about home and family change while he was away? Have you ever felt like running away? What would you miss about home?

3. What emotions did the father and his two sons express? What do you like about the older son? What's he going to do about the chip on his shoulder? Can you imagine these two brothers working together in the field after the celebration?

4. How is this father's love like God's love for us? What does it tell us about our relationship to others in our family?

ALL IN THE FAMILY

All families have tensions and problems that have to be worked out. Some problems are small and petty, others are big and serious. Building loving family relationships is hard work. How would you deal with these situations?

Whenever my friends come over to the house, my sister always acts hyper. It's so embarrassing.

The house always seems to be a mess. Why does Mom get so upset when I leave my books on the kitchen counter?

My dad is a health nut. How come there's never any **good** food in the house?

Ugh! My brother hasn't taken a shower or brushed his teeth for ages. I can't stand to look at him.

My older sister has announced she doesn't believe in God. "I can't help it, I just don't," she says.

My sister is going with a guy with a bad reputation. Doesn't she care what people think?

Mom wants the family to move to a different city so she can take a new job. What about me? Why do I have to leave my friends?

When Dad comes to my games, he makes a fool of himself yelling at the players and the referees. It's like he suddenly becomes a monster.

Mom is so strict about the music I want to listen to and videos I'd like to rent. Why can't she lighten up like other parents?

I hate going to church—it's so boring! But that doesn't seem to bother my parents. They make me go anyway.

How did you do? Did you find some of the situations tough? Sometimes families need the help of trained people in the church and community. And remember, God knows you. He knows and loves your family. And he hears and answers prayers about your family's needs.

18

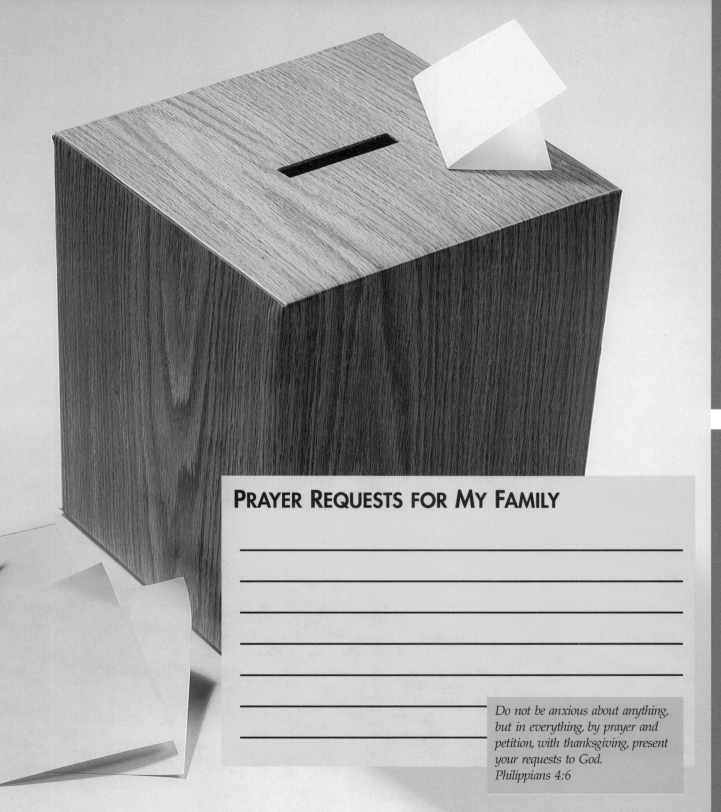

PRAYER REQUESTS FOR MY FAMILY

_____

_____

_____

_____

_____

_____

*Do not be anxious about anything,
but in everything, by prayer and
petition, with thanksgiving, present
your requests to God.
Philippians 4:6*

Friends Forever

DOUBLE TWIST

"What'cha doing?" Adam asked. His friend Brian sat hunched over a yellow form on his desk, scribbling intently.

"I'm filling out my housing application for summer band camp," Brian said. "I'm supposed to write down what I want in a roommate, and they'll assign me someone I'll like."

He made a final flourish with his pencil. "Or at least somebody I can stand for two weeks."

Adam picked up the application and slowly read it. "Says you want someone who's dishonest . . . surly . . . selfish . . . doesn't bathe much. . . . That sounds rotten! You really want to room with someone like that?"

"Not particularly," Brian admitted. "But there shouldn't be much competition for a surly kid who doesn't wash. That way I won't be disappointed when I don't get a really neat roommate.

"Besides," he added, "someone as crummy as I've described will make me look good by comparison."

Brian's logic has more twists than a bag of pretzels. . . .

You do . . . want to judge carefully when you start granting others influence on your life. Your friends will color your thinking and attitudes in many ways.

David Willingham, *Kings Don't Get Report Cards*, © 1995, CRC Publications

The pleasantness of one's friend springs from his earnest counsel.

Proverbs 27:9

Bad company corrupts good character.

1 Corinthians 15:33

✔ QUALITY CONTROL

When we buy clothes, books, tapes, food, CDs, and dozens of other things, we expect these products to meet our standards. If they don't, we're not satisfied. It's the same with choosing friends.

There are many different kinds of friends. We set friendship standards when we say

✓ "She's a friend."
✓ "He's *just* a friend."
✓ "She's a *good* friend."
✓ "He's my *best* friend."

What we are really saying is that to meet the test of friendship, our friends need to have certain qualities. If you were to choose a close friend, what qualities would this person have? Which of these qualities are the most important to you?

Following is a list of qualities you might want in a friend.
Rank them from 1 (least important) to 10 (most important).

1. _10_ My friend is someone I can *trust* in all situations.

2. _10_ My friend has *respect* for others and for me.

3. _2_ My friend has a *good sense of humor* and makes me laugh.

4. _7_ My friend *shares my interests* so we enjoy doing things together.

5. _10_ My friend is *generous* to me and to others.

6. _9_ My friend shares my *Christian values,* and it shows.

7. _6_ My friend *understands* my ups and downs.

8. _7_ My friend is *loyal* to me no matter what others say.

9. _1_ My friend is *talented* and appreciates my ability too.

10. _4_ My friend is a good *listener* and really hears me.

Which quality (or maybe more than one) did you rate a 10? Why? How do you measure up to these standards?

1. 7   7. 8
2. 9   8. 6
3. 8   9. 10
4. 9   10. 7
5. 10
6. 5

Love and a Bottle of Perfume

(Reading based on John 12:1-11)

Setting: The home of Lazarus in Bethany. It is six days before the Passover.

Speaker 1: I'm one of the people who's been invited to a dinner given in honor of Jesus of Nazareth. Lazarus is here too. What a miracle! It wasn't too long ago that he was lying dead in his grave, stone cold. I'll never forget the sight—Mary and Martha, Lazarus' two sisters grieving, Jesus crying with them and asking us to move the stone away from the tomb. And then the most amazing thing of all—Jesus prayed to God and called in a loud voice, "Lazarus, come out!" And there he stood in front of us—alive again! Is it any wonder that we want to honor Jesus, our friend?

Mary: *[speaking to herself]* I hardly know what I'm feeling any more! I'm so glad Lazarus is alive again, but now Jesus keeps telling us that *he's* going to die. Nobody seems to be thinking about that now. Maybe I just better go help Martha with dinner. But I can't stop thinking about Jesus—that's all that really matters to me. I don't care what other people think, I'm going to tell him now. What if this is my last chance to let him know how much I love him?

Speaker 2: Mary seems very excited about something. Wonder what's in that jar she's carrying? Look! She's pouring something over Jesus' feet—mmmm—smells great. Must be a really expensive perfume! And now she's wiping his feet with her hair! What's this all about?

Judas: *[to himself]* Ridiculous! That smell is too much. And what a waste of money! Why isn't this silly woman in the kitchen helping her sister?

Speaker 2: Judas looks pretty upset. And if I know Judas, he won't be the least bit afraid to say so.

Judas: What do you think you're doing, woman? Are you crazy? You could have sold this expensive perfume and given the money to the poor. That stuff must be worth at least a year's wages. What a waste!

Speaker 1: After Judas's outburst, we all look at Jesus. Everyone wonders what's really going on here. Does Jesus understand Mary? What about Judas—is he really so concerned about the poor?

Jesus: Leave her alone. It was intended that Mary should save this perfume for my burial, but she has chosen to honor me now. Judas, you will always have the poor to worry about, but I won't always be here with you. Mary's love will comfort me in the week ahead.

Speaker 2: Jesus' miracles are making the Jewish leaders very nervous. Now they're getting angry too. If Jesus keeps this stuff up, more and more Jews are going to follow him. The Roman leaders are afraid the people will want to make Jesus their king. I'm afraid there's trouble brewing. I've heard rumors about killing Jesus—and Lazarus too—my friends!

ON-LINE

1. What has happened in Jesus' life since he raised Lazarus from the dead?

2. What important Jewish religious celebration was about to occur? What meaning did this feast have for Jesus?

3. Why did Jesus say that the perfume was intended for his burial? Did Mary know something that the others at the dinner didn't seem to know?

4. How did Mary show her love for Jesus? Why was this gift so special? Why did she do it?

5. What can we do to show our love for Jesus? Why should we want to do these things?

25

WHAT A FRIEND WE HAVE IN JESUS

*What a **friend** we have in Jesus, all our **sins** and **griefs** to bear!*
What a privilege to carry everything to God in prayer!
*Oh, what peace we often forfeit, oh, what needless **pain** we bear,*
All because we do not carry everything to God in prayer.

*Have we **trials and temptations**? Is there **trouble** anywhere?*
We should never be discouraged; take it to the Lord in prayer.
*Can we find a friend so faithful, who will all our **sorrows** share?*
*Jesus knows our every **weakness**; take it to the Lord in prayer.*

*Are we **weak and heavy laden**, cumbered with a **load of care**?*
*Precious **Savior** still our **refuge**! Take it to the Lord in prayer.*
Do your friends despise, forsake you? Take it to the Lord in prayer!
*In his arms he'll take and shield you; you will find a **solace** there.*

Joseph M. Scriven, 1855

26

NOTES IN THE MARGIN

FROM ME . . . _____

_____

_____

_____

_____

TO YOU . . . I_____

_____

_____

_____

_____

Greater love has no one than this, that he lay down his life for his friends. You are my friends if you do what I command.

John 15:13-14

LESSON Four

Many Are One

America's not a blanket woven from one thread, one color, one cloth. When I was a child growing up in Greenville, South Carolina, and grandmother could not afford a blanket, she didn't complain and we did not freeze. Instead, she took pieces of old cloth—patches, wool, silk, gabardine, croker sack on the patches— barely good enough to wipe off your shoes with.

But they didn't stay that way long. With sturdy hands and a strong cord, she sewed them together into a quilt, and a thing of beauty and power and culture.

Jesse Jackson in *The American Reader* by Diane Ravitch, © 1990, *Harper Perennial*

CHOPSTICKS, FORKS, OR FINGERS?

People from many different *races* make up our North American society. Like the individual patches in a quilt, each race adds its own *culture* (customs, clothing, foods, religious beliefs and practices, language) to our society. Often we don't understand one another's culture.

Listed below are some everyday things people in North America do. Some things on the list are things everyone probably does. Other things are more often done only by people from a certain cultural background. Work with a partner and put a C in front of each thing that people from specific cultures might do.

____ Practice manners

____ Eat with chopsticks

____ Eat with a knife, fork, spoon

____ Laugh out loud at a joke

____ Lower eyes when talking to older people

____ Spend time with family

____ Celebrate Hanukkah

____ Wear a turban

____ Wear blue jeans

____ Eat bacon and eggs for breakfast

____ Eat tortillas for lunch

____ Learn a foreign language

____ Speak Vietnamese and English

____ Make turquoise jewelry

____ Work in a factory

When we learn to appreciate the beauty of each individual culture's "patch," we can create a design of harmony and beauty as we live and work together in God's world! As you complete the sentences below, think about the benefits of living in a society that is, in effect, a patchwork quilt.

- One way that I am different from other people is . . .

- The most interesting part about knowing people of other races is . . .

- Sometimes it's hard to accept people who are different from me because . . .

- One way that teens from every culture are alike is . . .

- The prejudice I see in my community is . . .

- The best way for Christians to deal with prejudice is . . .

BREAKING DOWN THE WALLS

READER'S THEATER
(BASED ON JOHN 4:1-26)

Setting: Samaria between Jerusalem and Galilee on the west side of the Jordan River.

Narrator: It's about noon, and Jesus is leading his disciples into Samaria near the town of Sychar. Samaria is a place most Jews go out of their way to avoid. Who'd want to be seen with those Samaritans, those half-Jews with such a strange religion? That well near the road was built by Jacob many years ago. Look, a Samaritan woman is coming to the well with a large jar to get water for her house. Two young people are sitting about twenty feet from the well, eating their lunch. One of them is Sasha, a sixteen-year-old Samaritan girl. The other is Toyvie, her brother. He's thirteen.

Toyvie: Sasha, don't those guys coming down the road look like Jews?

Sasha: Yes! They sure look hot and worn-out. Wonder what they want?

Toyvie: Who cares? What do you think they're doing here anyway?

Sasha: Who knows? Looks like the whole gang is heading for town—except for one. Look! He's talking to that woman at the well!

Toyvie: What's wrong with him? Doesn't he know a man doesn't talk to a woman who's alone . . . and especially that woman?

Sasha: Is that the woman Father told us about?

Toyvie: Yes, she's the one who's had all those husbands. She's always alone at the well—I think the other women avoid her.

Sasha: Do you think . . . yes, that guy's asking for a drink from Jacob's well!

Toyvie: Yeah! Just like a Jew! They preach about our unclean water jugs, but, boy, if they need a drink bad enough . . .

Sasha: Sssshhhh! Don't be so hateful. Besides, let's try to hear what they're saying . . .

Jesus: Hello! Will you give me a drink?

Woman: You are a Jew, and I am a Samaritan woman. How can you ask me for a drink?

Jesus: If you had any idea who you're talking to, you might have asked me for a drink of water, and I would have given you living water.

Woman: How is that possible? You don't even have a bucket, and the well is too deep.

Jesus: I have something different in mind. When you drink water from this well, you will be thirsty again, but there's also a kind of water that quenches your thirst so you'll never be thirsty again.

Toyvie: What's he talking about—living water? Who *is* he—some kind of magician?

Sasha: I'm not sure what he's saying either. Sounds like he's talking about something religious.

Woman: Sir, give me this water so I won't get thirsty and have to keep coming here day after day during the hottest time to draw water.

Jesus: Go call your husband and come back.

Woman: I have no husband.

Jesus: You are right when you say you have no husband. The fact is that you have had five husbands, and the man you now have is not your husband. What you have just said is quite true.

Toyvie: I can't believe it! He knows all about this woman, and he still talks to her.

Sasha: And not only is he talking to her, he sounds kind and caring! What's with this man?

Woman: Sir, I can see that you are a prophet. Our fathers worshiped on this mountain, but you Jews claim that the place where we must worship is in Jerusalem.

Jesus: Believe me, woman, a time is coming when you will worship the Father neither on this mountain nor in Jerusalem. You Samaritans worship what you do not know; we worship what we do know, for salvation is from the Jews. Yet a time is coming and has now come when the true worshipers will worship the Father in spirit and truth, for they are the kind of worshipers the Father seeks. God is spirit and his worshipers must worship in spirit and in truth.

Toyvie: Is this stranger saying that we Samaritans don't know what we're doing? That sounds just like a Jew.

Sasha: No, I think he's saying God doesn't care *where* we worship, he just cares about *how* we worship.

Toyvie: Well, just how are we supposed to worship?

Sasha: He says in the name of Jesus and in the power of the Spirit.

Toyvie: Why is this woman so eager to believe what he says?

Sasha: I'm not sure, but she really seems to trust him.

Woman: I know that the Messiah is coming. When he comes, he will explain everything to us.

Jesus: I who speak to you am he.

Toyvie: Did you hear that? He claims that he is the *Messiah!*

Sasha: Look! The woman is leaving without her water jar. Let's follow her into town. I've got to hear what she has to say!

Narrator: When the woman came into town and told others about her encounter with Jesus, many came to talk to him. They invited Jesus to stay. Jesus stayed for two days, talking to the people. And many believed in him.

ON-LINE

1. What barriers did Jesus break down when he talked to the Samaritan woman?

Find examples of each of these kinds of barriers Jesus broke down in today's Bible story:

- Cultural taboos (something you shouldn't do if you're from a certain culture)

- Prejudice (an unreasonable attitude of anger toward an individual or group of people)

- Superior attitudes ("I'm better than you")

2. Are these barriers still standing today? Think of examples close to home and some that describe our nation and our world.

3. What about us? How do our attitudes and actions sometimes set up barriers to friendship?

TAKE ME IN

When Phong Nguyen walked the halls at school, he felt like he was all alone. There were hundreds of kids talking and laughing, slamming locker doors and hurrying to their classes, but he was not part of the crowd. He was Vietnamese, and he liked to imagine that each day he was in Vietnam playing in the warm surf of the ocean with his friends or sitting around the fire with his family in their village. The stories his parents told of their life there made Phong feel like that's where he could fit in.

After the war Phong's father was desperate to get out of the country. He was a veteran of the South Vietnamese Army and had spent a year in jail for refusing to enter a post-war "re-education" camp. One night Phong's father and mother crowded into a boat with 168 other people to escape. After being robbed several times by pirates, the group finally arrived in Malaysia. People in the camp dreamed of going to America and talked about the security of being "taken in" there.

Was it really just a dream? Phong felt so left out, especially in school. History class was the worst. He wanted to ask, "Why does the textbook make the Vietnam War sound like such a waste? Doesn't anyone understand what happened to my family?" Phong found it hard to share his ideas when he felt so different from the other kids. Although Aaron, a husky, red-haired boy who sat in front of him, completely ignored him, Phong was sure Aaron's loud laugh was making fun of him. Kendra, a short, dark-haired girl, sat behind him. Kendra was a soccer player and track star. She was friendly, but Phong felt a little awkward talking to someone who was so popular.

One day as he was walking down the hall, Phong was stopped by the soccer coach. "I hear you're a good soccer player, Phong. Why don't you kick the ball around with us during open gym tonight?" the coach asked. Phong loved soccer, and he was pretty good at it too. He had thought about going out for the team, but he didn't know exactly what

to do or if the other boys would accept him. "All right," he said with a shy smile as he headed off for another history class.

His mind filled with images of soccer as he hurried to his seat. He didn't notice a large leg suddenly shoot out in front of him. He stumbled awkwardly over the leg and fell hard to his knees. "Watch where you're going, you dumb gook!" Aaron said with a big smirk on his face. Phong heard some snickers from a few other boys in the class. His knees ached with pain as he slowly tried to get up. He felt as though the whole class were watching him and laughing at his stupidity. "Aaron, what a jerk! Why don't you grow up and show some consideration for other people?" It was Kendra standing in the doorway, one hand on her hip, her face flushed with anger. The smile on Aaron's face vanished instantly, and his cheeks burned red with embarrassment.

Phong didn't say anything to Kendra as they both took their seats, but she tapped him on the shoulder and asked, "Are you okay?" "Yeah, I'm fine," he said with a grateful smile. He thought to himself, "Guess I'll take in the open gym tonight, maybe she'll be there too."

DIRECTIONS

In the column on the left, list the attitudes and actions that left Phong out. In the right column, list the attitudes and actions that took Phong in. Count up the number of items in each column. What's Phong's balance? More "outs" than "ins"? If you attended this school, would Phong be more "taken in" by you than he felt in the story?

LEFT OUT	TAKEN IN

34

IT MAKES NO DIFFERENCE

1 It makes no dif-ference who we are, what
2 It makes no dif-ference where we live, in
3 It makes no dif-ference how we look, what
4 It makes a dif-ference how we treat our

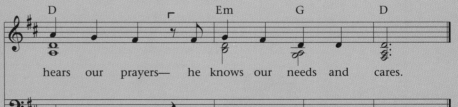

lan-guage we may speak;
ci-ty, town, or farm;
col-or is our skin;
neigh-bors and our friends;

Refrain

God loves us all and

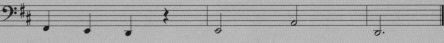

hears our prayers— he knows our needs and cares.

Optional endings

(cares.)

Words: Doris Clare Demaree; adapted by Bert Polman, 1993

Words © 1994, CRC Publications. Music © 1994, Sean E. Ivory.

Music: Sean E. Ivory, 1993

Music used with permission of Sean E. Ivory.

No matter what our age, or race, or color, we are the human family together, for the Creator made us all.

Our World Belongs to God, 12

I now realize how true it is that God does not show favoritism but accepts men from every nation who fear him and do what is right.
Acts 10:34-35

35

Choices

HONESTY AND ALL THAT STUFF

Share everything.
Play fair.
Don't hit people.
Put things back where you found them.
Clean up your own mess.
Don't take things that aren't yours.
Say you're sorry when you hurt somebody.
Wash your hands before you eat.
Flush.
Warm cookies and cold milk are good for you.
Live a balanced life—learn some and think some and draw
and paint and sing and dance and play and work every
day some.
Take a nap every afternoon.
When you go out into the world, watch out for traffic, hold
hands, and stick together.
Be aware of wonder.

From *All I Really Need to Know I Learned in Kindergarten* by Robert Fulghum. Copyright © 1986,
1988 by Robert L. Fulghum. Reprinted by permission of Villard Books, a division of Random House, Inc.

TUG-OF-WAR

We learn many of the rules and values of our culture from our parents and teachers as we grow up. We also learn about our culture and especially about what people value by listening to music, watching TV and movies, reading books and magazines. Sometimes the message we get from these sources is the opposite of what we hear at school or at home. This can create conflict—it's like playing tug-of-war.

Think about a movie or TV program you've watched recently. List some of the messages it gave you—use the words from the two Bible verses to help you decide which column the message fits.

CHRISTIAN MESSAGES

Whatever is true, whatever is noble, whatever is right, whatever is pure, whatever is lovely, whatever is admirable . . .
    Philippians 4:8

1.

2.

3.

4.

WORDLY MESSAGES

Evil thoughts, murder, adultery, sexual immorality, theft, false testimony, slander . . .
    Matthew 15:19

1.

2.

3.

4.

Try this same "conflict test" with the music you listen to or with the books and magazines you read. Which side is winning the tug-of-war for your values?

GOOD AND BAD?

Do not love the world or anything in the world. If anyone loves the world, the love of the Father is not in him. For everything in the world—the cravings of sinful man, the lust of his eyes and the boasting of what he has and does—comes not from the Father but from the world. The world and its desires pass away, but the man who does the will of God lives forever.
1 John 2:15-17

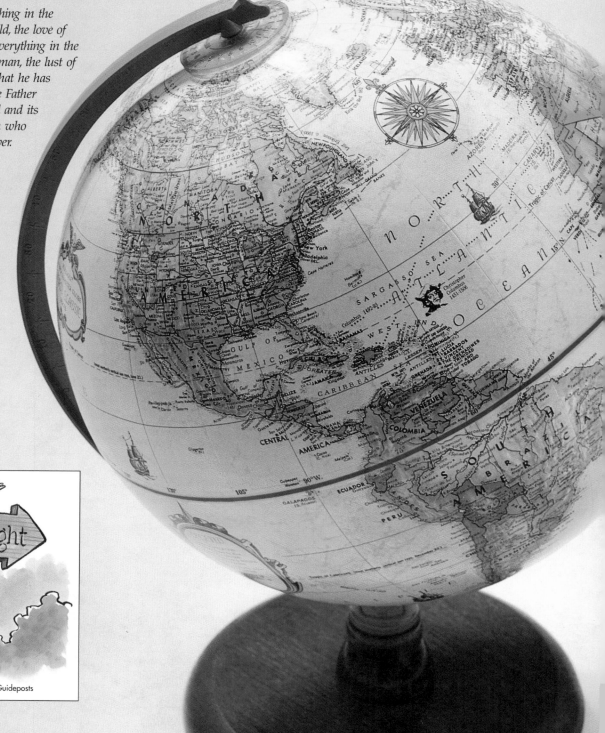

Directions to Heaven:

Turn Right

AND KEEP STRAIGHT

© Guideposts

ON-LINE

We live in a society that contains both good and evil. The big question is this: How can we live in this world and not let the bad part win us over? In the Scripture passage above, John, one of Jesus' disciples, gives us good advice.

1. Some things about our world are just plain bad. They are never good, always evil. Underline those that John mentions. Then add a few more to the list.

2. Name three things about this world that you really like—things that are good gifts from God. How can even these good things become bad?

3. What happens to the things of this world?

4. Being a Christian means learning to live in this world, to enjoy it without letting it become more important to us than Jesus. What can we do to accomplish this?

Pray every day make the right desijen

POP, ROCK, OR COUNTRY?

Music will always include a mixture of good and bad. It's good because it's created with notes, melody, and harmony, which are part of God's creation. . . . Music is bad, however, because it comes from the heart of people, and those hearts are bent.

Ken Heffner, "Teen Music," *The Banner,* Oct. 16, 1995

What influence does music have on our culture? On *you?* Look at the titles of these songs:

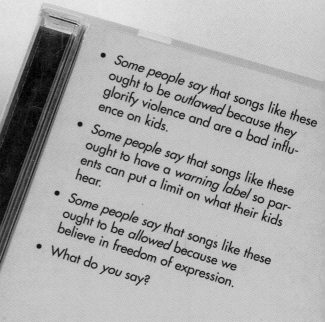

"Cop Killer" by Ice-T
(from *Body Count*)

"Red Light Special" by TLC
(from *CrazySexyCool*)

"Twenty Foreplay" by Janet Jackson
(from *Design of a Decade*)

"Geek Stink Breath" by Green Day
(from *Insomniac*)

"Momma's Gotta Die Tonight"
by Body Count

"I Saw Your Mommy [Dead]"
by Suicidal Tendencies

- Some people say that songs like these ought to be outlawed because they glorify violence and are a bad influence on kids.

- Some people say that songs like these ought to have a warning label so parents can put a limit on what their kids hear.

- Some people say that songs like these ought to be allowed because we believe in freedom of expression.

- What do *you* say?

LIGHTS

For you were once darkness, but now you are light in the Lord. Live as children of light (for the fruit of the light consists in all goodness, righteousness and truth) and find out what pleases the Lord.
Ephesians 5:8-10

Spirit of the living God,
*   fall afresh on me;*
Spirit of the living God,
*   fall afresh on me.*
Melt me, mold me,
*   fill me, use me.*
Spirit of the living God,
*   fall afresh on me.*

Text by Daniel Iverson, © 1926, Birdwing Music (ASCAP)

Christians are
the light of the world,
but the switch has to
be turned on.

Reprinted from *What on Earth Are You Doing, for Heaven's Sake?* © 1990, The C. R. Gibson Co. Illustration by Bron Smith. Used by permission.

41

LESSON

Six

Take Notice!

42

"ICE SCREAM BOY— A LAMENT"

Reader 1: Little boy, who are you? Little boy, who are you? . . .

Reader 2: Hungry for breakfast in mid-afternoon?
And all you want is an ice cream cone. . .
Macaroni and cheese for supper—
But Mom don't come home 'til 2 a.m.

Reader 1: Little boy, who are you? Little boy, who are you? . . .

Reader 2: Bareback in the rain?
Someone stole your shirt:
Ain't got no friends, nobody likes you.
You got no brothers or sisters? All alone.
And all you want is an ice cream cone.

Reader 3: Speak up, kid: the traffic's too loud,
I just can't hear ya 'bove the hum drum moan . . .
A cryin' face in a screamin' crowd—
And all you want is an ice cream cone.

Reader 2: At the city park all day,
Do you ever go home?
Making piggie banks from plastic cartons,
But you can't even buy an ice cream cone.

Reader 3: Speak up, kid: the traffic's too loud,
I just can't hear ya 'bove the hum drum moan . . .
A cryin' face in a screamin' crowd—
And all you want is an ice cream cone.

Reader 2: Hair hangin' down in your eyes,
Hiding your tears, cries for food . . .
Speak up, kid: the traffic's too loud . . .
And all you want is an ice cream cone . . .

Reader 1: Little boy, what are you? Little boy, what are you? . . .

© 1995 by Michael Brands. Used by permission.

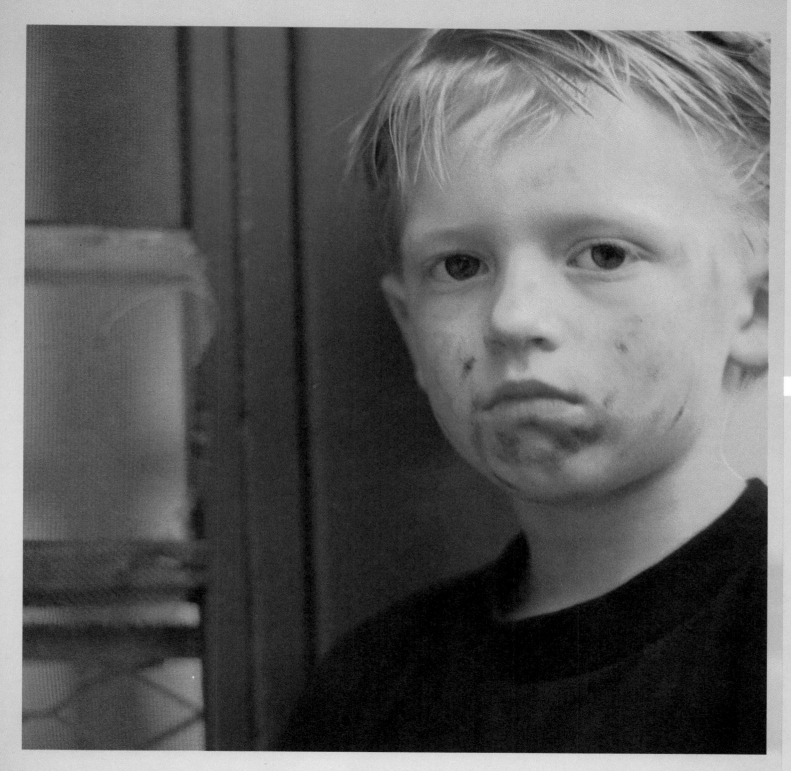

The Rich Man and Lazarus

19Once there was a rich man. He was dressed in purple cloth and fine linen. He lived an easy life every day. 20A man named Lazarus was placed at his gate. Lazarus was a beggar. His body was covered with sores. 21Even dogs came and licked his sores. All he wanted was to eat what fell from the rich man's table.

22The time came when the beggar died. The angels carried him to Abraham's side. The rich man also died and was buried. 23In hell, the rich man was suffering terribly. He looked up and saw Abraham far away. Lazarus was by his side. 24So the rich man called out, "Father Abraham! Have pity on me! Send Lazarus to dip the tip of his finger in water. Then he can cool my tongue. I am in terrible pain in this fire."

25But Abraham replied, "Son, remember what happened in your lifetime. You received your good things. Lazarus received bad things. Now he is comforted here, and you are in terrible pain. 26Besides, a wide space has been placed between us and you. So those who want to go from here to you can't go. And no one can cross over from there to us."

27The rich man answered, "Then I beg you, father. Send Lazarus to my family. 28I have five brothers. Let Lazarus warn them. Then they will not come to this place of terrible suffering."

29Abraham replied, "They have the teachings of Moses and the Prophets. Let your brothers listen to them."

30"No, father Abraham," he said. "But if someone from the dead goes to them, they will turn away from their sins."

31Abraham said to him, "They do not listen to Moses and the Prophets. So they will not be convinced even if someone rises from the dead."

Luke 16:19-31 NIrV

44

ON-LINE

The rich man in today's Bible story was blessed by God in two ways. He was given riches, and he had the Old Testament to tell him how to live. Yet he tried to excuse himself—he just didn't know! Do you "buy" it, or is ignorance no excuse? The verses from Luke 16:19-31 (p. 44) will help you think about this question—read the entire passage before you decide.

1. Explain the sin of the rich man—what exactly did he do wrong?

2. What two requests did the rich man make of Abraham? What did Abraham tell him?

3. What if this story were happening in your community today? Who would be the rich? The poor? What would be the "rich man's" excuse?

45

NO EXCUSES!

If I can stop one heart from breaking,
I shall not live in vain.
If I can ease one life the aching,
or cool one pain,
or help one fainting robin unto his nest
again,
I shall not live in vain.

Emily Dickinson, *The Complete Poems of Emily Dickinson,* © 1925,
Little Brown and Co. Used with permission.

He has told you what he wants, and this is all
it is: to be fair and just and merciful, and to
walk humbly with your God.
Micah 6:8, The Living Bible

46

The secret of living is the joy of giving.
You're probably thinking, "Give me a
break—what do I have to give?" Your
leader will help you plan a "give-away"
walk with God this week.

- Give away thanks.

- Give away forgiveness.

- Give away hope.

- Give away information.

- Give away compassion.

- Give away love.

Reprinted from the *Church Herald* October 1995.
Copyright © 1995 by *Church Herald* Inc. Used with
permission.

LOVE IN ACTION

*RIPON, Calif. Every one of the 265 kids
at Ripon Christian High School respond-
ed to a challenge to put Christian love in
action by spending an entire day doing
work projects in 31 locations in the near-
by communities of Ripon, Modesto, and
Stockton. . . .*

*Corey Hoekstra, a senior, said he and
seven other students agreed to help out at
Interfaith Ministries in Ripon. The boys
cut down trees and weeded gardens,*

*while the girls sorted clothes. He said
they had a great time working together.*

*A group of 15 students went to help out
a man in Sacramento who had sand-
bagged his riverside home during the
January floods. He needed help toting the
sand back to the river. Freshman Heidi
Summerfield said she and her classmates
spent the whole day wheelbarrowing sand
to the river. "It was fun to help people like
that," she said.*

School parent Ann Jean Vander Veen, of First Christian Reformed Church, Ripon, helped supervise a group of teens who worked at a daycare center for people with Alzheimer's disease. "We washed the van, weeded the premises, and played games with the patients," Vander Veen said.

"The kids learned firsthand what Alzheimer's is," she added. "I was impressed with their compassionate attitude."

Some kids spent the day painting over graffiti. One group painted an entire building. The owner of the building was so impressed with their handiwork that he bought pizza for all the kids. . . .

Freshman Cheryl Vennema helped landscape a children's crisis center. "I felt good about that," she said.

Three groups of students went to the Transitional Learning Center in Stockton, where they did a variety of chores, including yard work and testing children for kindergarten. At an interfaith center in Modesto, students bagged beans and unloaded bread, and at a convalescent home, students cleaned the kitchen, helped out at a birthday party, and gave patients wheelchair rides. Students also delivered flowers to patients at a hospice center, did filing at a Red Cross office, washed windows in a church, prepared food at a gospel center, and packaged articles at a Salvation Army center.

School counselor Peter Duyst said all the planning he and others did for the work day was worth the satisfaction they felt about the results. "The kids learned a lot about putting their Christianity into practice in a caring, loving way," he said.

Ruth Donker, *The Banner*, March 27, 1995, CRC Publications

Front and Center?

Don't push your way to the front; don't sweet-talk your way to the top. Put yourself aside, and help others get ahead.
Philippians 2:3, THE MESSAGE

DOUBLE VISION

Pride has a good side and a bad side. It is good for us to have a strong sense of self-esteem or to take pride in our appearance. Pride is bad when it becomes self-worship. It is wrong to love ourselves so much that we always want to be praised. It's wrong to put our own interests above the interests of others.

Sometimes it's difficult to draw the line between "good" and "bad" pride. With a partner, think about each of the following statements. If you both agree that a statement is an example of "good" pride, write a G in the blank next to it. If you both think that a statement is an example of "bad" pride, write a B in the blank next to it. Put a question mark in front of any statement on which you cannot agree. Be ready to defend your labels to the group.

_G_ I work hard for all the A's that I get in school.

_B_ I used to be proud, but now I'm as humble as can be.

_B_ I would never wear anything from Thrifty's—it's so cheap!

_B_ The only reason that I have a great body is because I work at it.

_G_ Kids really like me because they find me easy to talk to.

_G_ I'm good at math because I have a logical mind.

_B_ I am probably the best scorer on our team, but the other players hardly ever pass me the ball.

_G_ We live in a good neighborhood because everyone takes care of their house and yard.

_B_ My dad is rich because he works hard.

_B_ I'm sure our team will win the championship because the other teams in our district stink.

49

READER'S THEATER
BASED ON MATTHEW 20:20-28

MY TWO SONS

Narrator: Jesus had been preaching and healing in Galilee and in Judea. Large crowds followed him everywhere he went. Now he was walking to Jerusalem. Along the way he stopped with his twelve disciples to rest and pray. He reminded them for the third time that he was going to Jerusalem to die. Then the mother of James and John came to Jesus to ask a favor.

SCENE 1: A ROADSIDE REQUEST

James: Mother, what brings you out on the dusty road today?

Mother: I've come to ask the Master that favor we've talked about.

Jesus: Kind woman, what is it you want?

Mother: I know you are building your kingdom. I would be honored to have John sit at your right hand and James at your left hand—my two sons with you, the king!

Jesus: James and John, you don't know what you are asking! Do you understand what is going to happen to me? Can you suffer with me?

James and John: Master, we can.

Jesus: Yes, James and John, you will suffer with me; your work will be hard. But only my Father can choose who will be honored to sit at my right and left hand.

SCENE 2: THE MASTER'S REMINDER

Peter: [to the other disciples] Did you hear that? James and John want to be right beside the king!

Judas: Pretty proud, huh? Can't figure out why they think they rate so much better than the rest of us!

Jesus: Friends, we need to talk about this. See how everybody out there in the world is caught up in a rat race? They all try to scramble to the top so they can tell everybody else what to do. That's not how it goes with us. Want to be the greatest? Head for the bottom, my friends! Want to be front and center? Then be everybody's slave. Follow my lead. I didn't come down here to be pampered by you. I came to serve you all by giving up my life. So don't squabble about honor, just do my work.

ON-LINE

1. Was it a good idea for the mother of James and John to ask this favor of Jesus? Why or why not?

2. James and John had left everything to follow Jesus. Did they follow blindly? What didn't they seem to know about Christ's kingdom?

3. If you were one of the other disciples, how would you feel about this request? Why?

4. What are the lessons Jesus teaches his disciples and all of us?

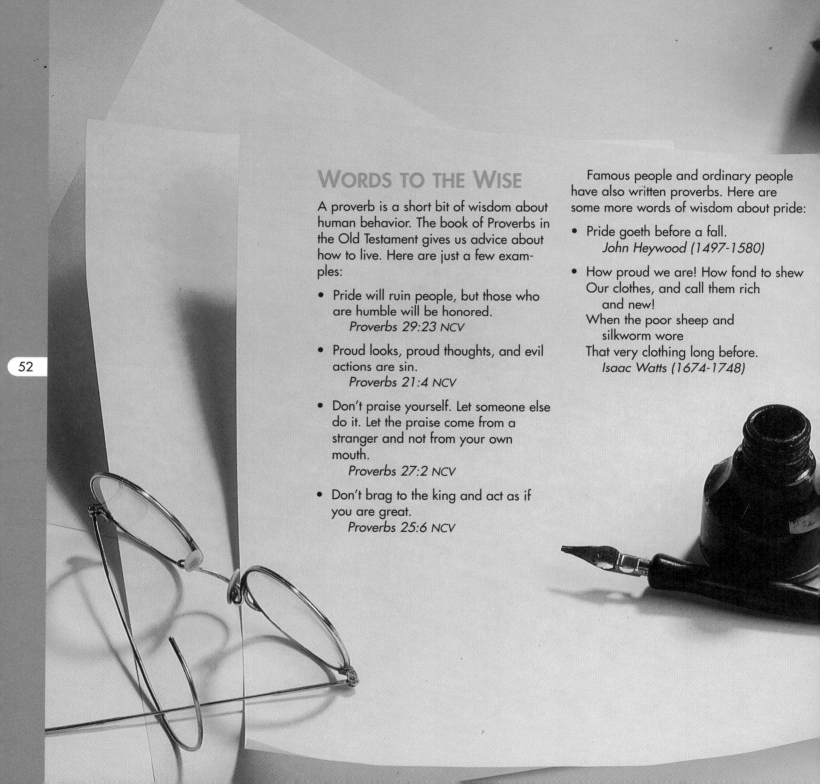

WORDS TO THE WISE

A proverb is a short bit of wisdom about human behavior. The book of Proverbs in the Old Testament gives us advice about how to live. Here are just a few examples:

- Pride will ruin people, but those who are humble will be honored.
  Proverbs 29:23 NCV

- Proud looks, proud thoughts, and evil actions are sin.
  Proverbs 21:4 NCV

- Don't praise yourself. Let someone else do it. Let the praise come from a stranger and not from your own mouth.
  Proverbs 27:2 NCV

- Don't brag to the king and act as if you are great.
  Proverbs 25:6 NCV

Famous people and ordinary people have also written proverbs. Here are some more words of wisdom about pride:

- Pride goeth before a fall.
  John Heywood (1497-1580)

- How proud we are! How fond to shew
  Our clothes, and call them rich and new!
  When the poor sheep and silkworm wore
  That very clothing long before.
  Isaac Watts (1674-1748)

YOUR TURN!

We have been studying the problem of sinful pride in our lives. With a partner, try to think of several short sayings that teach us something about pride and humility. Once you have several proverbs written, choose your favorite and make it into an attractive sign.

Here's a sample to help you get started:

> Wearing your halo too tight
> also gives others a headache.

Reprinted with permission from *What on Earth Are You Doing, for Heaven's Sake?* © 1990 by Guideposts, Carmel, NY 10512

Swallowing your pride is non-fattening.

Anonymous

PROVERBS:

_____

_____

_____

_____

_____

_____

More Stuff?

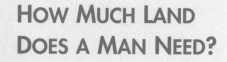

HOW MUCH LAND DOES A MAN NEED?

Pahom was a Russian peasant who did a good job farming his plot of land. Each year he plowed and sowed the soil, mowed hay, cut timber, and pastured his herd. Although his family had all they needed, Pahom was unhappy. His property was too small. He was jealous of the rich landowners who had lots of land.

One day Pahom's complaints came to the attention of the local ruler. He decided to make Pahom a special offer. Since Pahom was a good citizen who worked hard and took care of his land, the ruler would give him all the land he could circle on foot between sunrise and sunset.

But the ruler insisted that the peasant must be back exactly where he started by sunset. If he did not get back to the starting point on time, he would not get any land.

Very early in the morning of the appointed day, Pahom's neighbors and friends came to the starting place to watch. When the first rays of sunlight broke over the horizon in the east, Pahom started out. By breakfast time he guessed he had walked three miles, and he noticed that the land was better the further he went. Each time that he thought he might turn toward home, he said to himself, "Just a little farther." He decided he would keep going until noon.

Turning left at noon, he paused for a quick lunch. He counted—ten miles to go! But the heat! He walked faster, almost

breathless as the afternoon wore on—the sun was about to set.

Some of Pahom's friends ran out to encourage him. "Hurry, Pahom, you can do it! It's not too far now; you're almost there." Pahom ran and stumbled to the ground. He got up and ran some more and then stumbled again while the sun dropped lower and lower.

But to everyone's relief, Pahom staggered across the finish line with a minute to spare. He had circled a huge amount of property. Now all the land that he wanted was his.

"Good man!" cried the ruler. "You have acquired plenty of land!" But just then Pahom's legs gave way, and he fell forward. One of his friends ran to lift him up, but the blood was flowing from his mouth. Pahom lay dead!

Paraphrased from Leo Tolstoy, "How Much Land Does a Man Need?" *The Portable Tolstoy* ed. John Bayley, Maude's translation © 1978, Viking Penguin, Inc.

GET IT NOW!

"Life's a game. Those who have the most toys at the end win."

Greed sticks that motto on our hearts, not just on bumpers! Clever commercials and ads (and bumper stickers) encourage us to want more and more. It's hard to resist the idea that we can only be happy when we have all the good things money can buy.

- Why are teenagers working nights and weekends, maybe even giving up time from school and church activities?

- Why are businesses so interested in appealing to these teen spenders?

Imagine that you work for a bumper sticker company. Your assignment is to write clever slogans that encourage teens to "Get It Now." Better hurry, there's a deadline!

Now imagine that you've just barely made the deadline. You're feeling pretty clever . . . and tired . . . and crabby . . . and empty. As you plop into bed, homework still piled on the floor, you wonder if the slogan is really the kind of advice teens should pay attention to. Take heart—God's got some really valuable advice for us!

Check it out in these three "bumper stickers."

Proverbs 23:4

Luke 12:15

1 Timothy 6:10

YOU WANT IT?
TAKE IT!

The story of Naboth's vineyard and Ahab's greed recorded in 1 Kings 21:1-16 sounds like an R-rated movie. Read the passage from your Bible, and then, with a partner, act out one part of the story for the whole group. Imagine you are sharing the latest video with a friend.

- **1 Kings 21:1-3 (Bargaining)**
- **1 Kings 21:4-7 (Sulking)**
- **1 Kings 21:8-10 (Scheming)**
- **1 Kings 21:11-14 (Killing)**
- **1 Kings 21:15-16 (Taking)**

SCRIPT:

You Want It!

LOCATION

TAKE   SOUND

SCENE
DIRECTOR

CAMERAMAN

ON-LINE

1. In this Bible passage, King Ahab wants Naboth's vineyard for a vegetable garden. Was Naboth a fool for not accepting his offer? Why or why not?

2. How could a simple "I want it" turn into such a horrible neighborhood crime? Who were the guilty? The innocent?

3. Ahab's greed led to Naboth's death. Our own greed can injure or even destroy a valuable relationship. Give examples of how the following forms of greed can hurt people and break down relationships:

   - jealousy

   - discontent

   - selfishness

   - desire for attention

   - desire for power

"BUT I NEED IT!"

So what do *you* want for your birthday? If someone gave you a gift certificate and told you to buy ten things you really want, what would you buy? List them below.

1. _____
2. _____
3. _____
4. _____
5. _____
6. _____
7. _____
8. _____
9. _____
10. _____

Gift Certificate

Presented to _____
for $ _____
_____ dollars

It's easy to dream about the things we *want*. It's a lot harder to decide what we really *need*. Look at your list on page 60. Complete the following steps to help you choose between wants and needs.

- Circle anything on your list that you need to be healthy.

- Cross off anything on your list that you know your family would not want you to buy.

- Cross off anything on your list that you know your family cannot afford to buy.

- Star anything on your list that would help you to learn something new.

- Cross off anything on your list that you think will make you more popular with your friends.

- Cross off anything on your list that you would buy just because you saw an ad on TV.

- Put a heart in front of anything on your list you could share with someone else.

POP!

Trust Me!

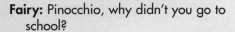

Fairy: Pinocchio, why didn't you go to school?

Pinocchio: School? Well, I . . . uh, I was going to school till I met somebody.

Fairy: Met somebody?

Pinocchio: Yeah! Uh . . . two big monsters. And . . . and they tied me in a big sack!

Fairy: You don't say!

Pinocchio: Look, my nose! What's happening?

Fairy: Perhaps you haven't been telling the truth. You see, Pinocchio, a lie keeps growing until it's as plain as the nose on your face.

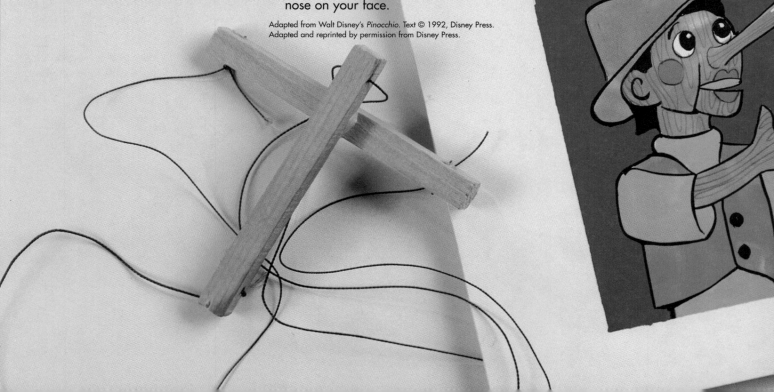

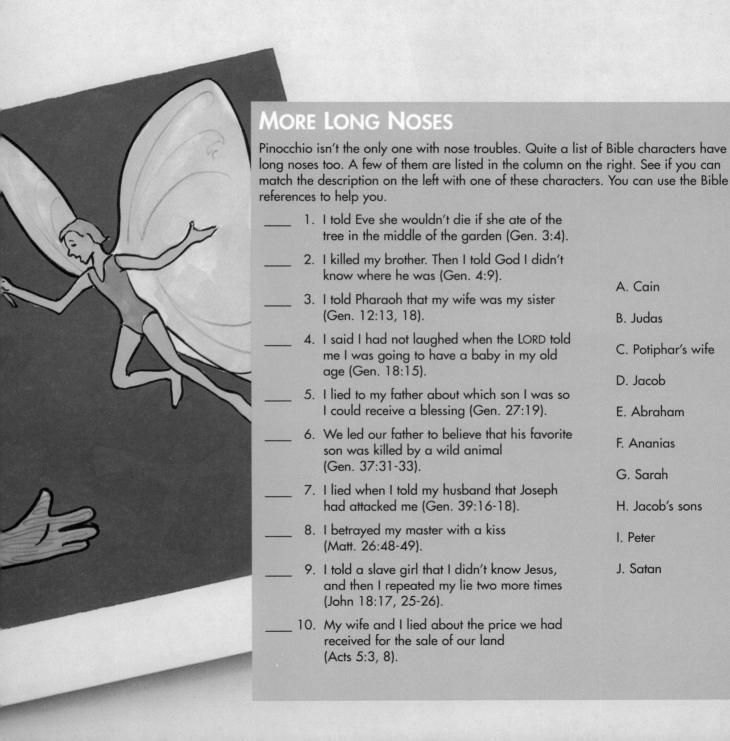

MORE LONG NOSES

Pinocchio isn't the only one with nose troubles. Quite a list of Bible characters have long noses too. A few of them are listed in the column on the right. See if you can match the description on the left with one of these characters. You can use the Bible references to help you.

____ 1. I told Eve she wouldn't die if she ate of the tree in the middle of the garden (Gen. 3:4).

____ 2. I killed my brother. Then I told God I didn't know where he was (Gen. 4:9).

A. Cain

____ 3. I told Pharaoh that my wife was my sister (Gen. 12:13, 18).

B. Judas

____ 4. I said I had not laughed when the LORD told me I was going to have a baby in my old age (Gen. 18:15).

C. Potiphar's wife

D. Jacob

____ 5. I lied to my father about which son I was so I could receive a blessing (Gen. 27:19).

E. Abraham

____ 6. We led our father to believe that his favorite son was killed by a wild animal (Gen. 37:31-33).

F. Ananias

G. Sarah

____ 7. I lied when I told my husband that Joseph had attacked me (Gen. 39:16-18).

H. Jacob's sons

____ 8. I betrayed my master with a kiss (Matt. 26:48-49).

I. Peter

____ 9. I told a slave girl that I didn't know Jesus, and then I repeated my lie two more times (John 18:17, 25-26).

J. Satan

____ 10. My wife and I lied about the price we had received for the sale of our land (Acts 5:3, 8).

BALANCING ACT

A lie is an untrue or inaccurate statement intended to mislead or deceive someone. Lying is something we choose to do. But even when we choose to speak the truth, knowing what to say is not always easy. To speak the truth in a loving way is a balancing act.

Don't lie to each other.
Colossians 3:9 NIrV

Just let your "Yes"
mean "Yes." Let your
"No" mean "No."
Matthew 5:37 NIrV

WHAT WOULD YOU SAY?

The words we speak should be true, but they should also be said with love. Think about these situations with a partner. Then decide together what you would you say. Be ready to explain your responses to the group.

- You are at a close friend's house for a pizza party. Suddenly, you find a hair just as stringy as the mozzarella in your slice.

- Your friend has terminal cancer. He's lost all of his hair, and his body is wasting away. When you go see him, he wants your opinion: "How do I look?" he says.

- Your best friend has asked you to go to a very popular R-rated movie. You know your parents would never approve. Your mom asks, "Where are you going tonight?"

- You're baby-sitting a small cousin. Before she leaves, your aunt says, "No friends." When she's gone, your best friend drops by and stays for an hour. When your aunt returns, she asks, "How did things go?"

- A good friend has a drug problem. You know he keeps a small amount of marijuana in his locker. You've told him that it bothers you, but he acts like it's no big deal. He says he's planning to quit. The principal takes you aside one day and tells you that she is really concerned about your friend. She wants to know if your friend has a drug problem or if he has any drugs in school.

- Your parents won't let you drive until you've taken driver's ed and gotten your permit. But just this once you decide to back the car out of the driveway so you can shoot some baskets. Crash! The mailbox is down.

We will speak the truth in love. We will grow up into Christ in every way.
Ephesians 4:15 NIrV

TWO LIES

¹Now a man named Ananias, together with his wife Sapphira, also sold a piece of property.

²With his wife's full knowledge he kept back part of the money for himself, but brought the rest and put it at the apostles' feet.

³Then Peter said, "Ananias, how is it that Satan has so filled your heart that you have lied to the Holy Spirit and have kept for yourself some of the money you received for the land?

⁴"Didn't it belong to you before it was sold? And after it was sold, wasn't the money at your disposal? What made you think of doing such a thing? You have not lied to men but to God."

⁵When Ananias heard this, he fell down and died. And great fear seized all who heard what had happened.

⁶Then the young men came forward, wrapped up his body, and carried him out and buried him.

⁷About three hours later his wife came in, not knowing what had happened.

⁸ Peter asked her, "Tell me, is this the price you and Ananias got for the land?"

"Yes," she said, "that is the price."

⁹Peter said to her, "How could you agree to test the Spirit of the Lord? Look! The feet of the men who buried your husband are at the door, and they will carry you out also."

¹⁰At that moment she fell down at his feet and died. Then the young men came in and, finding her dead, carried her out and buried her beside her husband.

¹¹Great fear seized the whole church and all who heard about these events.

Acts 5:1-11

ON-LINE

1. What exactly did Ananias and Sapphira do wrong? Why do you think they kept some of the money?

2. If you're wondering why Ananias and Sapphira were punished so severely, remember that this happened during the very early days of the church. Why was it so important that everyone be obedient and honest at this time? Do you think it's still important for the church today?

3. Just as dishonesty could break down trust in the early church community, so too it can break down our relationships today. Explain how dishonesty can harm the relationships between

   - a parent and child.

   - two close friends.

   - students and their teacher.

MY WORD

We want others to trust us, to depend on our word. We want our family and friends to believe that we're honest. The checklist below lists situations that might tempt us to be less than honest. Read each statement, and then check the box that fits how you would respond most of the time—"Always Honest" or "Sometimes Dishonest."

Always Honest   **Sometimes Dishonest**

I'm always honest/sometimes dishonest when

❏	❏	I tell friends how I feel about them.
❏	❏	I describe what I have been eating.
❏	❏	I explain how much homework I did after school.
❏	❏	I get asked about something I broke.
❏	❏	I borrow clothes or other things from my brother or sister.
❏	❏	I tell my parents where I am going or where I have been.
❏	❏	I protect a friend who's in trouble.
❏	❏	I am asked if I did my science project by myself.
❏	❏	I tell funny stories about myself to others.
❏	❏	I brag about something I just did.
❏	❏	I tell my parents how much money I spent.
❏	❏	I give a teacher an excuse for missing a test.
❏	❏	I return something to a store for a refund.
❏	❏	I explain why I can't go somewhere with a friend.
❏	❏	I say things to God in prayer.

- **Share** with a partner some situations that you checked "Always Honest." How does being honest in these situations help others know they can trust you?

- **Choose** one situation you would like to improve. How can you be truthful and loving in this situation?

69

- **Pray** for God's help to speak the truth in love and trust him! Are you learning to depend on Jesus?

"I am the way and the truth and the life."
John 14:6

Those who know your name will trust in you, for you, LORD, have never forsaken those who seek you.
Psalm 9:10

Short Fuses

SIZZLING

Cheryl tensed. Don had picked the wrong line at Jiffy Burger again. To the right and left, people were moving forward, getting their burgers and fries, and going merrily on their way.

Not their line. It was creeping ahead with the speed of a glacier. Had been for several minutes.

Cheryl glanced at Don. The little veins in his neck had begun to stand out. Next his face would turn red. Then he'd explode. She'd seen it before.

"What's wrong with these clowns?" Don muttered. "Don't they know how to count change?"

Cheryl stared straight ahead. Their cashier wore a bright yellow "Trainee" tag on her uniform.

"Be nice," Cheryl said. "Our cashier is new."

"So that's the problem." Don was louder now. His face was the color of a Swiss army knife. "They were really scraping the bottom of the barrel to hire Speedy up there."

Cheryl flinched. People in other lines were looking at them.

"I mean, it's not like you have to be a rocket scientist to ring up a few burgers." Don could probably be heard in the parking lot. "We could grow old and die waiting on Speedy."

The trainee cashier flushed. She fumbled with a new roll of quarters,

70

trying to break it open on the edge of her register drawer. The paper wrapper ruptured and coins skittered across the counter.

"That's it!" Don was making himself heard in the next time zone. "We'll be here all night if we wait on her!"

He spun and elbowed his way toward the door. Cheryl mumbled an apology to the man behind her and darted out with her eyes on the floor.

David Willingham, *One Large Order of Faith to Go,* © 1991 CRC Publications

"I'm Mad! OK?"

Yes! It's OK to feel angry. Anger is an emotion, a feeling inside us. That's how God made us. Most people have a hard time admitting they are angry. They think anger is sin, and a person who expresses anger is a bad person. That's not true! But it is true that we can sin if we express our anger in a way that hurts ourselves and others.

Go ahead and be angry. You do well to be angry—but don't use your anger as fuel for revenge. And don't stay angry. Don't go to bed angry.
Ephesians 4:26
THE MESSAGE

Get these out of here! How dare you turn my Father's house into a market!

John 2:16

The six situations on page 73 might cause us to feel angry. Add one or two sentences to the situation to finish the story. With a partner, think of reasons why you or someone else might be angry in each situation. Then decide together if it's OK to feel angry about this situation. (We'll talk about what to do with angry feelings a little bit later.)

SITUATION	I'M MAD BECAUSE . . . (GIVE ONE OR TWO REASONS.)	OK? (YES OR NO? WHY?)
You and your older brother are sharing the backseat on a family trip. Your brother . . .		
You're cheering wildly—your team's ahead by one point! The referee . . .		
You're watching a TV special about world hunger. The starving kids . . .		
You get home from school just as everyone else rushes in. Mom asks you to . . .		
You're at a party with friends. Everyone's saying Joe is . . .		
You open the garage door to get out your bike. Then . . .		

MEET JONAH

You're a reporter for "Streetside," a local television news program. You've just read a story in the local paper about Jonah. (Read Jonah 4 for the scoop!) He's definitely the guy to interview for your show, so you find the man and talk to him. Here's the sound track:

Reporter: Welcome to another "Streetside"! I've been roaming the streets of Nineveh today looking for a man named Jonah. I've finally found him sitting on the ground just outside the city. Let's get his story! Hello, Jonah, I'm a roving reporter with Channel 9.

Jonah: Get out of my face! Leave me alone!

Reporter: Whoa! Feeling a bit edgy today, are we?

Jonah: What's it to you, anyway? Hey, you're not one of these Ninevites, are you?

Reporter: No, sir, I'm just a reporter for "Streetside" on . . .

Jonah: [interrupting] Oh, lucky me! And in case you don't know, I'm just a minor Hebrew prophet.

Reporter: Yes, sir, I know.

Jonah: And don't call me "sir"! Jonah, that's my name. Prophecy, that's my game.

Reporter: And you've been bringing your prophecy to the people of Nineveh, right?

Jonah: You better believe it! I just got done warning these people that in forty days their precious city will be turned upside down.

Reporter: Really? And why is that, sir . . . I mean, Jonah?

Jonah: The place was full of sinners, and God was about out of patience.

Reporter: And you told the people that?

Jonah: You bet I did! I didn't want to, mind you, but the last time I tried to get out of it, I got thrown overboard from a ship and . . . [sighs] but that's another whale of a story!

Reporter: So, you told these Ninevites that God was ready to wipe them out. What did they do, start throwing eggs and tomatoes at you?

Jonah: Huh! That's what I expected. I thought they would run me out of the city like some wild dog foaming at the mouth with rabies.

Reporter: But they didn't?

Jonah: No, they didn't! The big chief began starving himself and praying. Then everyone else did too—just follow the crowd! Before I knew it, they were all feeling sorry for their sins.

Reporter: But . . . that's good!

Jonah: No! That's bad!

Reporter: Ah, I'm getting a little confused here. You're a prophet. You warn people about their sin and about how God is going to punish them. They do exactly what you say. You should be happy!

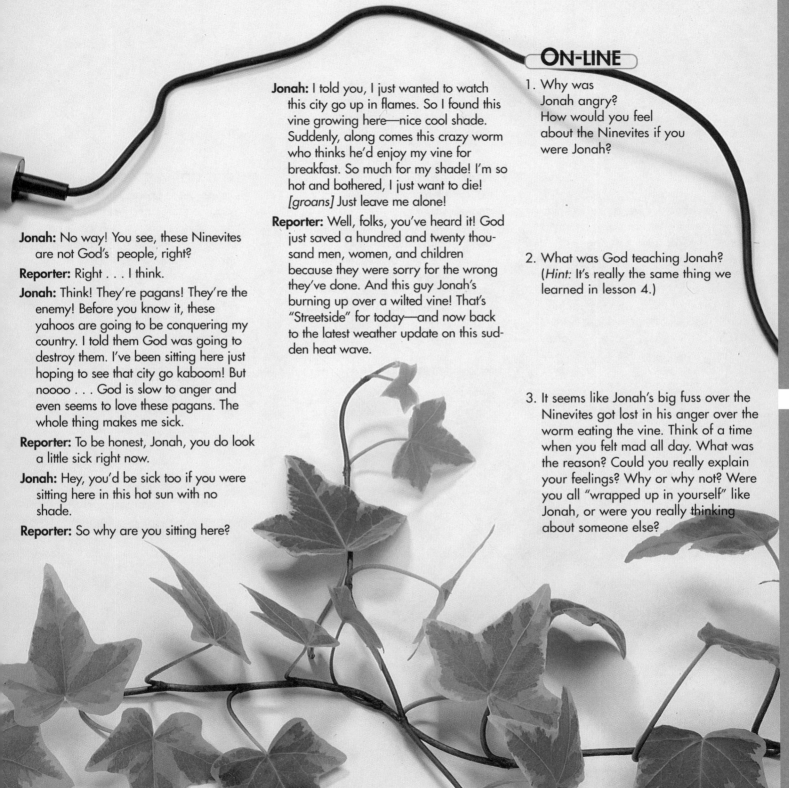

Jonah: No way! You see, these Ninevites are not God's people, right?

Reporter: Right . . . I think.

Jonah: Think! They're pagans! They're the enemy! Before you know it, these yahoos are going to be conquering my country. I told them God was going to destroy them. I've been sitting here just hoping to see that city go kaboom! But noooo . . . God is slow to anger and even seems to love these pagans. The whole thing makes me sick.

Reporter: To be honest, Jonah, you do look a little sick right now.

Jonah: Hey, you'd be sick too if you were sitting here in this hot sun with no shade.

Reporter: So why are you sitting here?

Jonah: I told you, I just wanted to watch this city go up in flames. So I found this vine growing here—nice cool shade. Suddenly, along comes this crazy worm who thinks he'd enjoy my vine for breakfast. So much for my shade! I'm so hot and bothered, I just want to die! [groans] Just leave me alone!

Reporter: Well, folks, you've heard it! God just saved a hundred and twenty thousand men, women, and children because they were sorry for the wrong they've done. And this guy Jonah's burning up over a wilted vine! That's "Streetside" for today—and now back to the latest weather update on this sudden heat wave.

1. Why was Jonah angry? How would you feel about the Ninevites if you were Jonah?

2. What was God teaching Jonah? (*Hint:* It's really the same thing we learned in lesson 4.)

3. It seems like Jonah's big fuss over the Ninevites got lost in his anger over the worm eating the vine. Think of a time when you felt mad all day. What was the reason? Could you really explain your feelings? Why or why not? Were you all "wrapped up in yourself" like Jonah, or were you really thinking about someone else?

75

NEXT TIME I'LL . . .

Some people "explode" when they're angry—like Don at Jiffy Burger. Others "sit on" their anger like Cheryl did. We may have learned these ways of expressing anger from our parents, our brothers and sisters, or even our friends. But there are healthier ways to express our anger. Here are three you can try:

- ### SAY IT!
  Use an "I" statement.

  Cheryl could have expressed her anger and the reason for it by saying something like this: "I'm angry (*feeling*) because you were rude (*reason*). Next time let's just talk while we wait" (idea for change).

  What could Don say? Try to think of an "I" statement that includes naming the feeling (anger), the reason for the anger, and an idea for change.

  _____

  _____

  _____

  _____

  _____

- ### HOLD IT BACK!
  Count to ten, take time out, go to another room.

  Imagine what would have happened if Don had held back his anger. Try retelling and acting out the scene at Jiffy Burger. This time Don holds back his anger. (If all else fails, send him down the street to McBurg's!)

- ### LET IT GO!
  Decide not to be angry or stay angry.

  Some things are just not worth getting angry about, or they can't be changed. Could Don do anything about the new cashier? Was waiting such a big deal? Pretend you're reading Don's mind, and he's deciding not to be angry. He's thinking . . .

  _____

  _____

  _____

  _____

  _____

  _____

  _____

Exercise adapted from the *Church Herald*, July/August 1995.
© 1995 by the *Church Herald Inc.* Used with permission.

THE QUARREL

I quarreled with my brother,
I don't know what about,
One thing led to another
And somehow we fell out.
The start of it was slight,
The end of it was strong,
He said he was right,
I knew he was wrong!

We hated one another.
The afternoon turned black.
Then suddenly my brother
Thumped me on the back,
And said, "Oh, come along!
We can't go on all night—
I was in the wrong."
So he was in the right.

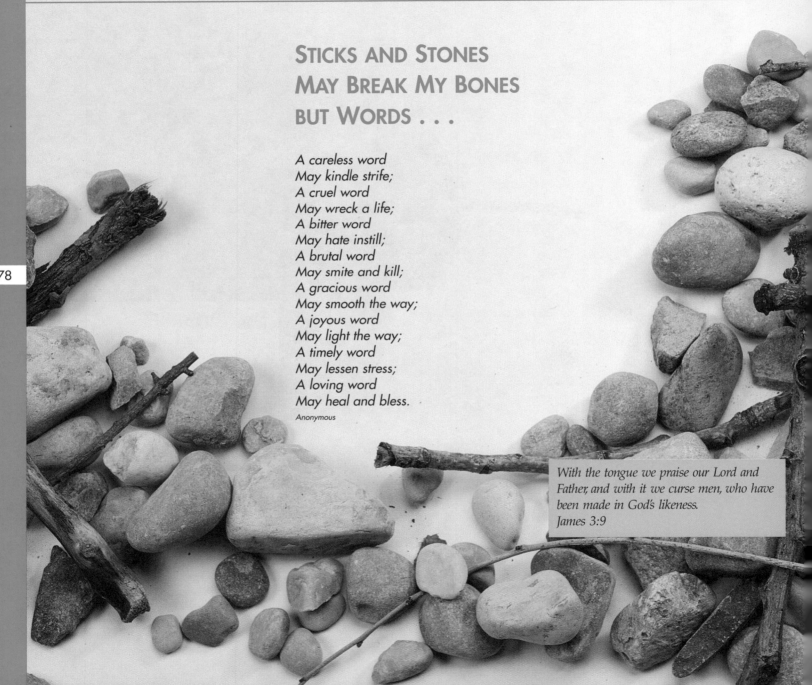

Just a Flashy Coat?

STICKS AND STONES
MAY BREAK MY BONES
BUT WORDS . . .

A careless word
May kindle strife;
A cruel word
May wreck a life;
A bitter word
May hate instill;
A brutal word
May smite and kill;
A gracious word
May smooth the way;
A joyous word
May light the way;
A timely word
May lessen stress;
A loving word
May heal and bless.
Anonymous

With the tongue we praise our Lord and Father, and with it we curse men, who have been made in God's likeness.
James 3:9

Wanted: Reporter.
Today's Headlines.
Weekend Shift.

Imagine that you are a reporter for your local newspaper. Your job is to cover the weekend police beat and the emergency room at the hospital. What reports of violence do you expect to come from homes? From schools? From neighborhoods? In the spaces below, write headlines for the stories you might hear in each of them.

• **Home Front**

• **School Patrol**

• **Neighborhood Watch**

But I tell you that anyone who is angry with his brother will be subject to judgment.
Matthew 5:22

ME TOO?

The headlines are full of examples of violence. It's hard to understand why these things happen. But have you ever wondered if your own words and deeds could lead to violence? Complete the following exercise as you think about that question. Circle the word from the columns on the left that best describes you.

Often   Sometimes   Never   1. I get very upset and angry when my parents won't let me do what I want.

Often   Sometimes   Never   2. When my brothers or sisters bug me, I hit or shove them.

Often   Sometimes   Never   3. I "blow up" at school about all the rules.

Often   Sometimes   Never   4. When someone is mean to me, I dream of ways to get even.

Often   Sometimes   Never   5. I hang around with kids who think it's OK to break the law.

Often   Sometimes   Never   6. I don't trust people whose skin is a different color than mine.

Often   Sometimes   Never   7. I watch movies and play computer games that have lots of violence.

Often   Sometimes   Never   8. I use bad language when I don't get my way.

Often   Sometimes   Never   9. I keep my anger bottled up inside—until I "explode."

Often   Sometimes   Never   10. I lose my temper over little things.

80

All spheres of life—
marriage and family,
work and worship,
school and state,
our play and art—
bear the wounds of our rebellion.
Sin is present everywhere—
in pride of race . . .
in abuse of the weak and helpless . . .
in destruction of living creatures. . .
We have become victims of our own sin.
Our World Belongs to God, 17

What a proud peacock you are, Joseph!
Genesis 37:10

"THE DREAMER"

It's just a "flashy" coat Dad gave me. Genesis 37:3

Did the wolves devour the sheep too? Genesis 37:33

Let's sell him cheap! Genesis 37:28

Looks like the green-eyed monster's got a hold on them! Genesis 37:11

But God sent me ahead of you to preserve for you a remnant on earth and to save your lives by a great deliverance. So then, it was not you who sent me here, but God. Genesis 45:7-8

ON-LINE

1. Bad feelings within a family can lead to violence, as we see in Joseph's story (Gen. 37). Explain how everyone's feelings played a part in what happened.

   • Jacob's feelings

   • Joseph's feelings

   • The brothers' feelings

2. If the brothers were on trial for murder and you were the judge, would you find them guilty? What evidence would you use?

3. Violence causes deep hurts that can last a long time. How did Jacob react to the news that Joseph had been killed by a wild animal? What effect did the abuse he suffered have on Joseph? On his brothers during all the years that passed before they were reunited?

4. The apostle Paul suffered pain and persecution. But through it all, he praised God, "the Father of compassion . . . who comforts us in all our troubles" (2 Cor. 1:3-4). Joseph must have felt this way too. How can we know that God cares about us when we experience trouble?

God has made me forget all my trouble.
Genesis 41:51-52

GOD IS WALKING
ME THROUGH

Never comes down as expected—
In sometimes mysterious ways.
How my heavenly Father surrounds me—
Goes before.
He is there in each moment unfolding.
Every treacherous step I must take.

Chorus:
God is walking me through—
And making me sing.
He's turning my whole world around
With the joy that He brings.
He's breaking my fall—
Lifting me up.
Changing my heart's point of view,
God is walking me through.

Peace at the height of confusion,
Calm in the worst of my fears,
Not a victim to life's circumstances—
All the wayward chances.
There's a reason for each disappoint-
ment.
And a rainbow above every cloud.
I will say outloud:
Chorus

It's ever the same—
The pleasure and pain in every life.
But count mine as gain
To walk in His light.
Chorus

83

Twelve

A New Life

BEING MADE NEW

[9]*You have gotten rid of your old way of life and its habits.* [10]*You have started living a new life. It is being made new so that what you know has the Creator's likeness. . . .*

[12]*You are God's chosen people. You are holy and dearly loved. So put on tender mercy and kindness as if they were your clothes. Don't be proud. Be gentle and patient.* [13]*Put up with each other. Forgive the things you are holding against one another. Forgive, just as the Lord forgave you.*

[14]*And over all of those good things put on love. Love holds them all together perfectly as if they were one.*

[15]*Let the peace that Christ gives rule in your hearts. As parts of one body, you were appointed to live in peace. And be thankful.*

[16]*Let Christ's word live in you like a rich treasure. Teach and correct each other.* [17]*Do everything you say or do in the name of the Lord Jesus. Always give thanks to God the Father through Christ.*

Colossians 3:9-10, 12-17 NIrV

▶ ON-LINE ◀

Today's Bible study is about living a new life: changed, growing, thankful. Let's find these three key points in the passage from Colossians 3.

- We've **changed!**
  Circle the words in verse 9 that tell how we've changed.

- We're **growing!**
  Underline all the words in verses 10, 12-14 that describe how we are growing to be more like Jesus.

- We're **thankful!**
  Draw a box around all the words in verses 15-17 that tell us what to do to show our thanks to God for giving us new life.

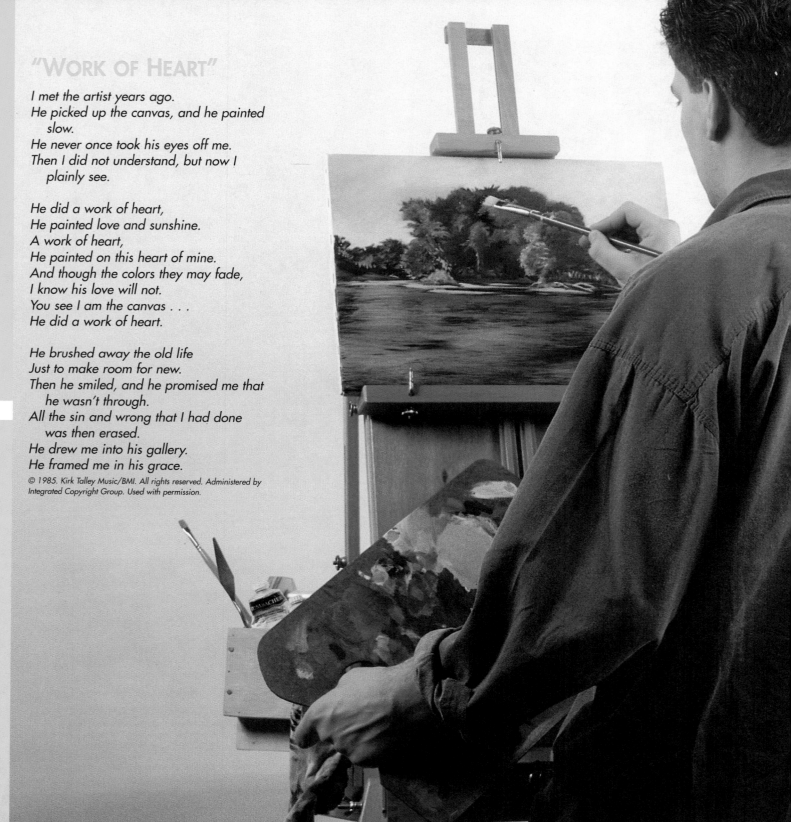

"WORK OF HEART"

I met the artist years ago.
He picked up the canvas, and he painted
*   slow.*
He never once took his eyes off me.
Then I did not understand, but now I
*   plainly see.*

He did a work of heart,
He painted love and sunshine.
A work of heart,
He painted on this heart of mine.
And though the colors they may fade,
I know his love will not.
You see I am the canvas . . .
He did a work of heart.

He brushed away the old life
Just to make room for new.
Then he smiled, and he promised me that
*   he wasn't through.*
All the sin and wrong that I had done
*   was then erased.*
He drew me into his gallery.
He framed me in his grace.

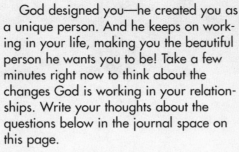

God designed you—he created you as a unique person. And he keeps on working in your life, making you the beautiful person he wants you to be! Take a few minutes right now to think about the changes God is working in your relationships. Write your thoughts about the questions below in the journal space on this page.

- How is God changing how you feel about yourself?

- What changes have you seen in your close relationships with others?

- What changes would you really like God to make in you and in your relationships with your family and friends?

MY THOUGHTS

1.

2.

3.

Jesus became wiser and stronger. He also became more and more pleasing to God and to people.
Luke 2:52 NIrV

PAY ATTENTION!

Sometimes we forget that Jesus grew up just like any other person. He grew in every way as we do: mentally (wiser), physically (stronger), spiritually (more pleasing to God), and emotionally (more loving).

Imagine that you're a member of a team of experts who write an advice column for teens. With the other members of your team, think about what advice you'd give them for growing in each of the four areas we've mentioned. As a team, write a sentence telling teens how to grow in each of the four ways. You want them to pay attention to growing in every area of life!

PAY ATTENTION: OUR ADVICE

1. Grow Mentally (learn more about God's world)

2. Grow Physically (develop healthy bodies)

3. Grow Spiritually (know and love God)

4. Grow Emotionally (love and serve others)

THANK YOU, LORD!

Loving God and others—that's what living a new life in Christ is all about. *You* are *being made new* if you believe that Jesus died for you. If you know his love, thank him for his "work of heart" in your life. If you don't know Jesus as your Savior, he invites you to ask him into your life! Write your prayer in the journal space on this page.

MY PRAYER

Dear Loved Ones,

I pray that he will use his glorious riches to make you strong. May his Holy Spirit give you his power deep down inside you. Then Christ will live in your hearts because you believe in him. And I pray that your love will have deep roots. I pray that it will have a sound foundation. May you have power with all God's people to understand Christ's love. May you know how wide and long and high and deep it is. And may you know his love, even though it can't be known completely. Then you will be filled with everything God has for you.

In Christ's love,

Paul

Ephesians 3:16-19 NIrV

Through My Father's Eyes

FROM MONDAY TO SATURDAY

MONDAY

Read Psalm 139. Thank God all day long for the wonderful way he made you—think of at least one thing you really like about yourself. Look at what God sees in you, his creation, and sing his praises.

TUESDAY

Read 1 Samuel 16:1-13. Often we just see what's on the outside of other people, and others see what's on the outside of us. But God has other ideas—he looks beyond the surface. He knows what we're really like. If that sounds a bit scary, remember that God loves us even though we're not perfect. That's exactly why he sent Jesus to save us from our sins.

WEDNESDAY

Read 2 Chronicles 30:1-5, 17-26. Maybe you've sung the lines "Just as I am . . . I come" from the well-known hymn. It's easy to give up on ourselves and think we'll never make it as a Christian. But God wants us to come just as we are to worship and serve him. We don't have to wait until we're grown up, until we know more about the Bible, until we get rid of our temper, until anything else.

THURSDAY

Read Luke 19:1-10. Zacchaeus didn't exactly "measure up"! But when Jesus spent time with him, he changed. That's the secret to our relationships with others. How can your family and friends tell that you know Jesus?

FRIDAY

Read Jeremiah 1:4-9. Just as God knew Jeremiah before he was born and had a plan for his life, God knows you and has a plan for your life. The Lord said to Jeremiah (and to you), "Do not say, 'I am only a child.'" Ask God to help you serve him today and to prepare for a lifetime of serving him with the gifts he's given you.

SATURDAY

Read Ephesians 2:10. We are God's creation, his masterpiece. And he already has work planned for us to do—there's no unemployment in God's business, no room for "I can't."

MEMORY WORK

Dear friends, let us love one another, for love comes from God.
1 John 4:7

91

Family Ties

TWO

FROM MONDAY TO SATURDAY

MONDAY

Read Psalm 107:4-9, 43. God's people have been prodigal sons and daughters for generations, but the "great love of the LORD" (v. 43) never fails. He'll lead you too! Ask your parents to share some examples of this leading in their lives.

TUESDAY

Read Numbers 12. Do you ever feel like you have a "Moses" in your life—the older brother with all the talents, the younger sister with all the brains? Sibling rivalry can really keep us from developing and using our own gifts to serve God.

WEDNESDAY

Read 2 Kings 21:1-9. Developing your independence from your parents is an important part of growing up. Think carefully about the things that really matter to your heavenly Father, and most likely your parents won't feel they're raising a "rebel"—most of the time anyway!

THURSDAY

Read Psalm 22:9-11, 24. You know that God placed you in a particular family for a purpose. Sometimes families face troubles (day-to-day problems or major crises that cause stress and even family breakdown). When troubles happen in your family, seek the loving help of others and trust God to walk with you.

FRIDAY

Read Exodus 1:1-7. Wow! What a clan Jacob's family was! Family ties give us something to hang onto in a crazy world (like Jacob's Egypt). Take time today to thank God for your parents and grandparents, for building memories that remind you that you belong.

SATURDAY

Read Mark 3:31-35; Luke 8:19-21. Was Jesus "cutting the apron strings"? As much as Jesus loved his earthly family and commands us to honor and obey our parents, he reminds us that membership in God's spiritual family is even more important. We're all God's adopted children, if we only believe in Jesus, God's Son.

MEMORY WORK

Dear friends, let us love one another, for love comes from God. Everyone who loves has been born of God and knows God.
1 John 4:7

Friends Forever

FROM MONDAY TO SATURDAY

MONDAY

Read Psalm 38:11; Job 19:19; Luke 22:61. How does it feel when your friends desert you when the going gets tough? Or maybe you've been the fickle one when someone really needed your loyalty. Isn't it great to know that Jesus is always faithful? He keeps his promise to be our friend forever.

TUESDAY

Read Proverbs 14:20; 19:4; James 2:1-9. It can become a habit to pick our friends by what they have, what they wear, what they can afford to do for fun. Snobs and cliques leave others out, and that's a lonely place to be at school or church or anywhere. Jesus has room in his circle of friends for everyone, rich and poor alike. How big is your circle?

WEDNESDAY

Read Proverbs 16:28; 17:9; James 5:19-20. Talking on the phone and hanging around together are fun ways to get to know your friends better. But when the talk turns to gossip, we're bound to hurt someone who probably could use a bit of extra friendship to get through a hard day. Remember, Jesus knows what that hurt feels like—the Jews had plenty of untruths to say about him!

THURSDAY

Read Proverbs 22:24; 29:22. What's your first reaction when friends and family members irritate you? Blowing up over everything that upsets us seldom changes much. Try the cooling effect of a kind word on a hot temper—it works like ice cubes in boiling water! Picture Jesus' love melting our hearts just like that—feel his calming presence.

FRIDAY

Read Job 29:4. Can't you feel the warmth of God's "intimate friendship" in Job's words? "Best" friends can often make us feel warmly accepted, but even the best of friendships have down times. It's not that way with Jesus—he knows us, he loves us always and forever, as no one else ever can! Even if we don't always feel close to God, he's close to us. How close did you move toward him today?

SATURDAY

Read John 14:25-27; 15:14-17. The Holy Spirit will help us to do what Jesus commands: Love each other. He's already given his life for us. Do you know the peace of that gift in your life now? Have you thought about professing your faith publicly?

MEMORY WORK

[7]*Dear friends, let us love one another, for love comes from God. Everyone who loves has been born of God and knows God.* [8]*Whoever does not love does not know God, because God is love.*
1 John 4:7-8

95

Many Are One

FROM MONDAY TO SATURDAY

MONDAY

Read Luke 9:51-56. Samaritans and Jews didn't have much use for each other. Because the Samaritans dismissed Jesus as one of those Jews who insisted on worshiping in Jerusalem, they missed the opportunity to meet the Son of God in person! And James and John were ready to call for a burst of flame to consume them. Jesus, though, shows patience with all of them—no favoritism!

TUESDAY

Read Matthew 15:21-28; Mark 7:24-30. Was Jesus discriminating against this Greek woman when he told her that the gospel was to be given first to the Jews? It's true that he came for the Jews, but he also came to save *all* who trust in him as this Greek woman did. She would be satisfied with even a "crumb" of Jesus' love—and he gives so much more!

WEDNESDAY

Read Jonah 3. Even after the whale-of-a-ride lesson, Jonah just couldn't accept the Ninevites. Sometimes we're just like Jonah. We know what God wants us to do, and sometimes we even do some pretty good things. But then the old feelings deep inside just come popping out again. We're better off letting God decide who's "out" and who's "in."

THURSDAY

Read Exodus 2:15-21. Moses got around! He was born a Hebrew and raised as a royal Egyptian. And when he escaped to Midian, he was a total stranger, a loner, but that didn't stop him from helping others. Then, before he knew it, Moses found himself welcomed into a Midianite home. Is someone new to your school or neighborhood? Reach out today!

FRIDAY

Read Matthew 12:1-8; Mark 7:1-13. Christians from other cultures have traditions that are different than ours. Jesus reminds the Jewish leaders that all the religious rules in the world won't really matter if we don't honor God's command to love each other. If we do that, it doesn't matter if we serve the same God differently.

SATURDAY

Read Matthew 9:35-38; Mark 6:34. In a world full of people, it's easy to feel lost in the crowd. You wonder if anybody notices you. Jesus does. He's like a shepherd who keeps track of each lamb in his care.

MEMORY WORK

[7]*Dear friends, let us love one another, for love comes from God. Everyone who loves has been born of God and knows God.* [8]*Whoever does not love does not know God, because God is love.* [9]*This is how God showed his love among us: He sent his one and only Son into the world that we might live through him.*
1 John 4:7-9

Choices

FROM MONDAY TO SATURDAY

MONDAY
Read 1 Kings 15:8-15. King Asa didn't have godly parents, but he chose to follow God. Even if generations of our parents and grandparents have been Christians, we've got the same choice to make. Do you have a role model?

TUESDAY
Read Exodus 32:1-6, 25-26. Talk about a bad case of peer pressure! Aaron let the crowd convince him to build the golden calf instead of standing up for what was right. Feel any conflict between your values and the crowd you want to be with? Maybe a little mountain time with God would give you the courage, like Moses, to rally your friends to the Lord!

WEDNESDAY
Read Daniel 3. Daniel's three friends really trusted God. They knew their God could save them from the fiery furnace. So they disobeyed the king's orders. Remember, kings and things will all pass away, but our God is forever!

THURSDAY
Read James 3:13-18. Contrasts! Choices! That's what living in this world is all about. A "me-first" attitude doesn't come from God. Check your relationships for signs of heavenly wisdom—"pure, peace-loving, considerate, submissive, full of mercy, impartial, sincere."

FRIDAY
Read 1 Kings 18:20-40. "Double-minded" is a good word to describe the people of Israel. Sometimes it's hard to be absolutely for or against something, but when it comes to choosing between the one true God and idols made by humans, only one choice is ever right. Ever wonder why it was so hard for the Israelites to figure that out? Even more amazing is God's choosing us. He gave his Son to prove it!

SATURDAY
Read Psalm 150. Everything we do can bring praise to God. Find out where (v. 1), why (v. 2), how (vv. 3-5), and who (v. 6) in this psalm. Then praise him in your own way.

MEMORY WORK

[7]Dear friends, let us love one another, for love comes from God. Everyone who loves has been born of God and knows God. [8]Whoever does not love does not know God, because God is love. [9]This is how God showed his love among us: He sent his one and only Son into the world that we might live through him. [10]This is love: not that we loved God, but that he loved us and sent his Son as an atoning sacrifice for our sins. 1 John 4:7-10

99

Take Notice!

FROM MONDAY TO SATURDAY

MONDAY

Read Psalm 73. Think of Lazarus lying at the gate of the rich man every day. It must have seemed to him that God was blessing those who didn't even love him and punishing those who knew him. But verse 18 tells us that God lets the wicked run on a "slippery slope"—get the picture? The rich man slid right into hell, money and all. How about you? Been running uphill lately serving the Lord, or just slipping along?

TUESDAY

Read James 2:5-9. James must have been thinking of the story his brother Jesus told about the rich man when he wrote this advice. Snubbing others because they're poor isn't just something that happened in Jesus' day. Ever been the kid who didn't have the "right" shoes or money for the game everyone's talking about? Why do we sometimes put dollar signs on people's faces?

WEDNESDAY

Read James 2:14-18. Problems like hunger and homelessness are so big. It's easy to shrug our shoulders, maybe even say a prayer and drop a dollar or two in the offering plate. It's true that we can't solve the whole problem, but we can do something. Share God's love—pass it on!

THURSDAY

Read Amos 7:10-17. "I'm just a kid!" Ever use that as an excuse? Amos let everyone know that he was just a shepherd, but God took him from his flock and said, "Go!" Maybe you're scared to visit someone with AIDS or serve at a soup kitchen. But remember this: God says, "Go—I'll be there too." Ready?

FRIDAY

Read Jeremiah 1:1-10. God knew Jeremiah before he was born and when he was "only a child." And God called him and touched him and promised to be with him. Think about it—Jeremiah was probably only about fourteen when God called him. Listen! God's calling you to serve him too.

SATURDAY

Read James 2:20-23, 26; 1 John 3:18. Love's got to act. God's given you love, forgiveness, and the promise of living forever with him. He's given his only Son. How's your give-away plan going this week?

MEMORY WORK

7Dear friends, let us love one another, for love comes from God. Everyone who loves has been born of God and knows God. 8Whoever does not love does not know God, because God is love. 9This is how God showed his love among us: He sent his one and only Son into the world that we might live through him. 10This is love: not that we loved God, but that he loved us and sent his Son as an atoning sacrifice for our sins. 1 John 4:7-10

Front and Center?

Seven

FROM MONDAY TO SATURDAY

MONDAY

Read Isaiah 39. King Hezekiah was a proud man and just couldn't resist the chance to show off his collection of riches to his visitors. He may have impressed a few Babylonians that day, but they had the last laugh when they carried off all this loot for themselves.

TUESDAY

Read Numbers 12:1-8. Looks like Aaron and Miriam had a bad case of sibling rivalry. God set them straight, though, by choosing Moses, who "was a very humble man," to be the leader. Firstborn or last born, leader or follower, we're all called to be servants.

WEDNESDAY

Read Luke 9:46-50. The disciples arguing? Once again, the question of who's #1 comes up. What does Jesus do? He tells these grown men to think of themselves as little children! Trying to be first in the kingdom will get you nowhere, in fact, Jesus says those who are "least among you all—[are] the greatest." So don't get caught in the "me-first" trap—it's a dead end.

THURSDAY

Read James 4:7-10. "Me first" is the devil's banner—an attitude that can fly about as high as a kite without a string. If you really want to soar, try a little humility. It's like hanging onto a helium balloon. So, since God's got the power to lift you up—why worry about it?

FRIDAY

Read Luke 24:13-35. James and John knew Jesus and they knew a little about his kingdom. But their pride kept them from knowing the whole story about Jesus. The men walking to Emmaus didn't really see Jesus until he broke the bread. Jesus has given us his Word and his Spirit to remind us of who he is and how we are to live. Are you walking with him?

SATURDAY

Read Psalm 145. Falling on our faces hurts our pride. But God picks us up and is "loving toward all he has made." "Great is the LORD!" Is he first, the greatest, in your life?

MEMORY WORK

[7]Dear friends, let us love one another, for love comes from God. Everyone who loves has been born of God and knows God. [8]Whoever does not love does not know God, because God is love. [9]This is how God showed his love among us: He sent his one and only Son into the world that we might live through him. [10]This is love: not that we loved God, but that he loved us and sent his Son as an atoning sacrifice for our sins. [11]Dear friends, since God so loved us, we also ought to love one another.
1 John 4:7-11

More Stuff?

FROM MONDAY TO SATURDAY

MONDAY
Read James 4:1-6. James may have been thinking about King Ahab when he wrote,"You kill and covet, but you cannot have what you want" (v. 2). It's easy to point our fingers at Ahab, but James reminds us that we often ask for things for the wrong reasons too. What do you want? Why?

TUESDAY
Read James 5:1-5. Moth-eaten clothes, rusty coins, burning flesh—that's the picture James paints for the wealthy who grab and hang on to their money. Jesus gives the solution: "But store up for yourselves treasures in heaven, where moth and rust do not destroy, and where thieves do not break in and steal" (Matt. 6:20). What kind of treasures does Jesus want you to "store up"?

WEDNESDAY
Read Psalm 23:1-3. The majority of North Americans seem caught up in the mad rush of earning money to buy more things—more wants. Compare the feeling of rushing around all day with the peaceful scene in these verses. Then find a quiet spot today to just think about Jesus and how he leads you, guides you, restores you. Why worry when you can pray?

THURSDAY
Read Numbers 18:8-10, 20-24. The Levites were Old Testament pastors, and they were "paid" with 10 percent of the gifts the Israelites brought to the temple. Although God doesn't ask for a dime of every dollar we earn, giving to his work is a way to thank him for his love. The things we have are gifts to use for caring for God's world and his people. Clink! Thanks, Lord!

FRIDAY
Read Numbers 28:1-15. An offering is an act of worship. God told the people of Israel he wanted this worship to be from the heart. "To love him with all your heart, with all your understanding and with all your strength, and to love your neighbor as yourself is more important than all burnt offerings and sacrifices" (Mark 12:33). Got your offering?

SATURDAY
Read Luke 7:11-16. Imagine how thankful the widow in Nain was to Jesus for giving back her son. He's given us life too—first he created us, and then he died to save us forever. Try counting the ways he's helped you today!

MEMORY WORK

[7]Dear friends, let us love one another, for love comes from God. Everyone who loves has been born of God and knows God. [8]Whoever does not love does not know God, because God is love. [9]This is how God showed his love among us: He sent his one and only Son into the world that we might live through him. [10]This is love: not that we loved God, but that he loved us and sent his Son as an atoning sacrifice for our sins. [11]Dear friends, since God so loved us, we also ought to love one another.
1 John 4:7-11

Trust Me!

FROM MONDAY TO SATURDAY

MONDAY

Read Luke 22:1-6. It's hard to imagine why Judas would turn against Jesus, but this passage tells us that Satan entered Judas. What if you had overheard the conversation between Judas and the chief priests? What would you have said to Judas? To Jesus?

TUESDAY

Read Luke 22:54-62. We know Peter was bold and sometimes loud. But a liar? Why didn't Peter get up and hide after he was asked just once if he knew Jesus? How do you think Peter felt when Jesus looked straight at him?

WEDNESDAY

Read Luke 22:66-71. Jesus told the council of elders, "I am the Son of God." That was enough for them to condemn him. If you had been one of the council members, would you have believed Jesus?

THURSDAY

Read Luke 23:13-25. Even though Pilate believed Jesus was innocent, he didn't have the courage to stand up for the truth. What do you think of the deal Pilate made with the crowd?

FRIDAY

Read Luke 24:1-12. The disciples didn't believe the women who tried to tell them that Jesus was alive. They were so sure Jesus was dead, they could hardly believe otherwise. Is it ever hard for you to believe it too?

SATURDAY

Read Luke 24:45-53. Jesus patiently reminded his disciples that he'd been telling them the truth all along about why he came. Now he promised them that he would send his Spirit. They knew they could trust Jesus when he said, "I am with you always." Are there others you can depend on to keep their word like that?

MEMORY WORK

[7]Dear friends, let us love one another, for love comes from God. Everyone who loves has been born of God and knows God. [8]Whoever does not love does not know God, because God is love. [9]This is how God showed his love among us: He sent his one and only Son into the world that we might live through him. [10]This is love: not that we loved God, but that he loved us and sent his Son as an atoning sacrifice for our sins. [11]Dear friends, since God so loved us, we also ought to love one another.
1 John 4:7-11

Short Fuses

FROM MONDAY TO SATURDAY

MONDAY

Read John 2:13-16. Jesus had a good reason for getting angry. Sometimes we have good reasons too—and sometimes we don't. Keep track of the things that make you feel angry this week. Try to sort out the reasons for your anger too. Ask yourself, Is it OK to be mad about this?

TUESDAY

Read Luke 22:47-53. Peter probably should have counted to ten first. Instead he let his anger guide his action—he cut off the high priest's ear. So Jesus called a time-out and healed the man's ear. This week, take a little time out with Jesus yourself!

WEDNESDAY

Read James 1:26; 3:7-8. Sometimes it's a good idea to say you're angry. But it takes practice to do that without spouting hot-tempered words. Sometimes our tongues are as out of control as a horse without reins. Try telling your mom or dad, "I'm angry because. . . ." You may be surprised at their reply.

THURSDAY

Read James 1:19-20. "Be quick to listen, slow to speak and slow to become angry" (v. 19). That's good advice. Think about an argument you've had this week—did you get angry right away? James says listen first! It may be tough to just sit there and hear somebody tell their side first, but it's worth a try.

FRIDAY

Read James 3:17-18. We're supposed to be *peacemakers*. That means acting like we have been changed by God. In your relationships, as you connect with family and friends this week, make peace. Put others first. Listen. Care. Do you feel the anger disappear in the locker room? At supper time? Thank Jesus for helping you to be more like him.

SATURDAY

Read James 5:13-16. Sometimes we hurt people when we're angry. Or they hurt us. James says, "Confess your sins to each other and pray for each other so that you may be healed" (v. 16). Are you in trouble with anyone this week? Telling someone you're sorry might feel a little funny, but it might just make your weekend. While you're at it, don't forget to thank Jesus for forgiving us all our sins!

MEMORY WORK

[7]Dear friends, let us love one another, for love comes from God. Everyone who loves has been born of God and knows God. [8]Whoever does not love does not know God, because God is love. [9]This is how God showed his love among us: He sent his one and only Son into the world that we might live through him. [10]This is love: not that we loved God, but that he loved us and sent his Son as an atoning sacrifice for our sins. [11]Dear friends, since God so loved us, we also ought to love one another.
1 John 4:7-11

Just a Flashy Coat?

FROM MONDAY TO SATURDAY

MONDAY
Read Exodus 20:13 and 1 John 3:15. God has given us his commandments as a guide for living. We break his command when we hate others. It's easy to let anger turn into hate that just won't go away. If you're hanging on to some angry feelings, talk to someone who can help you. And ask for God's love to take away the hate and hurt.

TUESDAY
Read Proverbs 3:31; 16:29; 24:1-2. It's hard to imagine envying "a violent man." Who'd want to be like that? But sometimes we follow the lead of a person who seems to control others. Where can you go for help when you feel pulled into a group that could cause trouble? Thank God for good friends who care!

WEDNESDAY
Read Proverbs 10:6; 11. Blessings and life—God's promise to those who love one another. Take time today to count the good things that happened to you because someone spoke words of love rather than hate. And then give some of them away so your family and friends have blessings to count too.

THURSDAY
Read 1 John 4:20-21. We can't love God if we don't love others. That's it, plain and simple. If we say we love God, that love *must* show in how we love others. Does anyone around you need love? Reach out to someone who wonders if God really cares. You can be God's "heart and hands" because his love is in you.

FRIDAY
Read Luke 6:27-28. It's easy to love those who love us. But Jesus wants us to love those who hate us and mistreat us. That can seem impossible, especially if we've been badly hurt. But God knows about broken relationships, and his love can work a miracle in every heart. He'll hear your prayers and use your good deeds!

SATURDAY
Read Ecclesiastes 9:1; Romans 8:28. Do you ever worry about the future? We don't know what will happen to us, but we do know that we are in God's hands. God is still "designing" us to be his masterpiece, always loving us and calling us to live for him. Love him with all your heart, and love others like yourself.

MEMORY WORK

[7]Dear friends, let us love one another, for love comes from God. Everyone who loves has been born of God and knows God. [8]Whoever does not love does not know God, because God is love. [9]This is how God showed his love among us: He sent his one and only Son into the world that we might live through him. [10]This is love: not that we loved God, but that he loved us and sent his Son as an atoning sacrifice for our sins. [11]Dear friends, since God so loved us, we also ought to love one another. [12]No one has ever seen God; but if we love one another, God lives in us and his love is made complete in us.
1 John 4:7-12

111

A New Life

FROM MONDAY TO SATURDAY

MONDAY

Read Mark 1:29-34. Jesus came to heal the sick and the lost. He cares about our bodies and our souls. What can you do to take care of your body? What can you do to grow spiritually?

TUESDAY

Read Luke 10:38-42. Jesus knew Martha had work to do around the house, but he wanted her to spend some time with him. He knows you're busy too with schoolwork and all the other things you like to do. It's good to be involved in lots of different things. But Jesus wants to spend some time with you too. Got a minute right now?

WEDNESDAY

Read Luke 6:43-45. Apple trees grow apples. Grapevines grow grapes. Good people "grow" good from good hearts. Good hearts are possible only when Jesus works in them. Do your words and actions remind others that Jesus is doing a "work of heart" in you?

THURSDAY

Read Galatians 5:22-25. More fruit! The Spirit will produce "love, joy, peace, patience, kindness, goodness, faithfulness, gentleness and self-control." Share a "handful" of this fruit with your family and friends today and feel the love of God growing in you.

FRIDAY

Read Psalm 51:10-13, 15. When God works in our hearts and saves us through Jesus, his Son, he sends his Spirit to give us joy. He opens our mouths to praise him. Do you know Jesus as your Savior? Then thank him every day for his love!

SATURDAY

Read Psalm 145. God keeps his promises. He never stops loving us. Through Jesus, you're *connected* to God! What a relationship! Praise him.

MEMORY WORK

7Dear friends, let us love one another, for love comes from God. Everyone who loves has been born of God and knows God. 8Whoever does not love does not know God, because God is love. 9This is how God showed his love among us: He sent his one and only Son into the world that we might live through him. 10This is love: not that we loved God, but that he loved us and sent his Son as an atoning sacrifice for our sins. 11Dear friends, since God so loved us, we also ought to love one another. 12No one has ever seen God; but if we love one another, God lives in us and his love is made complete in us.
1 John 4:7-12

113